Willie Hill

13 - Welch Hall

German Review
and Practice

German
Review
and
Practice

C. R. Goedsche and *Meno Spann*
NORTHWESTERN UNIVERSITY

AMERICAN BOOK COMPANY

Preface

German Review and Practice is intended for use during the first term of the second or intermediate year of instruction. Part One, Forms and Structure, reviews the essentials of grammar. Part Two, Aids for Reading, presents idioms and syntactical constructions that are most troublesome for the student. Part Three, Aids for Speaking and Writing, focuses on various semantic problems in oral and written expression. All three parts offer extensive practice material.

Since the student ought to be introduced to literary readings at the beginning of his intermediate year of study, we propose that the book be used as a companion to literary texts. Thus the grammatical elements in Part One need not be taken up in the order presented. Particular points of grammar can be reviewed as the need arises. Part Two, however, should be studied systematically and thoroughly early in the term, since mastery of these items will help the student considerably in developing his reading skill.

Our suggestions for the use of this text make it unnecessary to devote the first term to lengthy grammar review. They also explain why we did not introduce each chapter by a reading passage. There is an additional advantage. Since we were not restricted to the limited and specific vocabulary of such reading selections in the preparation of exercises, we were able to offer more and truly functional practice sentences.

A separate Student Manual, *German Oral Practice*, provides extensive and intensive audio-lingual exercises reinforced by a comprehensive tape program. The Manual has perforated pages and blank spaces so that it can serve also as a student workbook for writing practice.

C.R.G.
M.S.

Contents

Part One: *Forms and Structure*

Part Two: *Aids for Reading*

Part Three: *Aids for Speaking and Writing*

Part One | *Forms and Structure*

1. Der-Words

MASCULINE	FEMININE	NEUTER	MEANING
der	die	das	*the*
dieser	diese	dies (dieses)	*this, that*
jeder	jede	jedes	*every*
mancher	manche	manches	*many a*
PLURAL: manche			*many, some*
solcher	solche	solches	*such a*
PLURAL: solche			*such*
jener	jene	jenes	*(that), the former*
welcher	welche	welches	*which*

2. Declension of Der-Words and Unpreceded Adjectives

SINGULAR

	MASCULINE	FEMININE	NEUTER
NOM.	(der Tee) dieser Tee	(die Milch) diese Milch	(das Wasser) dieses Wasser
	kalter Tee	kalte Milch	kaltes Wasser
GEN.	(des Tees) dieses Tees	(der Milch) dieser Milch	(des Wassers) dieses Wassers
	kalten Tees	kalter Milch	kalten Wassers
DAT.	(dem Tee) diesem Tee	(der Milch) dieser Milch	(dem Wasser) diesem Wasser
	kaltem Tee	kalter Milch	kaltem Wasser
ACC.	(den Tee) diesen Tee	(die Milch) diese Milch	(das Wasser) dieses Wasser
	kalten Tee	kalte Milch	kaltes Wasser

PLURAL

NOM.	(die Getränke)	diese Getränke (*beverages*)
		kalte Getränke
GEN.	(der Getränke)	dieser Getränke
		kalter Getränke
DAT.	(den Getränken)	diesen Getränken
		kalten Getränken
ACC.	(die Getränke)	diese Getränke
		kalte Getränke

Observe:

a. die Milch, die Getränke; BUT: **diese** Milch, **diese** Getränke; **kalte** Milch, **kalte** Getränke;

das Wasser; BUT: **dieses** Wasser; **kaltes** Wasser.

The **-ie** and **-as** in the definite article become **-e** and **-es.**

b. der Geschmack **dieses** Tees; BUT: der Geschmack **kalten** Tees;

die Temperatur **dieses** Wassers; BUT: die Temperatur **kalten** Wassers.

The genitive singular of an unpreceded adjective is rarely used; and the ending **-en,** deviating from the **-es** ending of the genitive singular masculine and neuter, normally occurs only in printed or written German.

EXAMPLES:

Der Becher ist voll **süßen** Weines.	*The cup is full of sweet wine.*
Sei **guten** Mutes!	*Be of good courage.*
Der Geschmack **frischen** Wassers.	*The taste of fresh water.*

3. Peculiarities of Form and Meaning of Der-Words

a. Die Koffer sind im Zimmer.
The suitcases are in the room.
Die Koffer sind in **dem** Zimmer.
The suitcases are in that room.
Die Koffer sind in **dem** Zimmer **da.**
The suitcases are in that room there.
Kennen Sie **den?**
Do you know that man?
Kennen Sie **die?**
Do you know that woman?
Bringen Sie **die** drei **da** auf Zimmer 14.
Take those three (suitcases) there to room 14.

Der and **die** may mean *that man* or *that woman* or any masculine or feminine noun that is to be pointed out. A man buying a hat (**der Hut**) might say:

Zeigen Sie mir **den** (*or*) **den da.**
Show me that one (or) that one over there.

b. The singular of **solcher** is rarely used; **so ein** or **solch ein** takes its place:

So (solch) einen Reiseführer gibt es nicht.
There isn't such a guide book.

c. The German demonstrative **jener** is rarely used; the definite article with or without **da** is used instead (see **a** above). **Jener** is not the equivalent of the English demonstrative *that*. It has the meaning of *that* only in elevated style or in poetry:

Da droben auf **jenem** Berge, da steht ein goldnes Haus.
Up there on yonder mountain there stands a golden house.

d. Dieser and **jener** express *the latter* and *the former:*

Dr. Meier und Dr. Alexis haben das Experiment besprochen. **Dieser** hält es für wichtig, **jener** für wertlos.
Dr. M. and Dr. A. have discussed the experiment; the latter considers it important, the former worthless.

e. The form **dieses** is not used as a complement of **sein;** use the short form **dies** or **das:**

Dies (das) ist mein Zimmer.   *This is my room.*
Dies (das) sind unsere Zimmer.   *These are our rooms.*

4. Differences between English and German in the Use of the Definite and Indefinite Articles

a. German has no definite article in the following expressions:

zu Beginn des Jahres	*at the beginning of the year*
gegen Ende der Woche	*toward the end of the week*
Anfang Januar	*at the beginning of January*
Mitte Februar	*in the middle of February*
Ende März	*at the end of March*
gegen Osten	*toward the east*
Wir waren **bei Müllers.**	*We were at the Müllers.*

b. English has no definite article in the following expressions:

little Hans	**der kleine Hans**
modern Germany	**das moderne Deutschland**
on Humboldt Street	**in der Humboldtstraße**
before breakfast	**vor dem Frühstück**
after lunch / dinner	**nach dem Mittagessen / Abendessen**
on Monday	**am Montag**
during supper	**beim Abendessen**
in July / spring	**im Juli / Frühling**
in school	**in der Schule**
in town	**in der Stadt**
to church	**zur Kirche**
to school	**zur Schule**
by train / car / airplane	**mit dem Zug / Wagen / Flugzeug**
for example	**zum Beispiel**

c. English uses the indefinite article, German the definite article:

3 marks a pound   3 Mark **das Pfund**

20 pfennigs a piece	20 Pfennig **das Stück**
She receives 100 marks	Sie erhält 100 Mark
a week / a month / a year.	**die Woche / den Monat / das Jahr.**
We drove 100 kilometers	Wir sind 100 Kilometer **die Stunde**
an hour.	gefahren.
She writes me once a week /	Sie schreibt mir einmal **die Woche /**
a month / a year.	**den Monat / das Jahr.**
as a rule	**in der Regel**
for a change	**zur Abwechslung**

d. English uses a possessive adjective with parts of the body or articles of clothing; German uses the definite article when the noun is not modified by an adjective:

Put it into your pocket.	Steck es **in die Tasche!**
He opened his eyes.	Er öffnete **die Augen.**
I have something in my eye.	Ich habe etwas **im Auge.**
But: *He opened his blue eyes.*	Er öffnete **seine blauen Augen.**

Exercises

E.1 *Insert the following der-words:* **der, dieser, jeder, welcher, der da** *as the meaning of a sentence permits. So that you may concentrate just on der-words, the genders of nouns are indicated as follows:* Mann (m); Frau (f); Kind (n). *A few common prepositions requiring the dative are used:* **aus, in, mit, von:**

1. Wie heißt _____ Herr (m)? 2. _____ Dichter (m) hat das gesagt?
3. Wie heißt _____ Dame (f)? 4. _____ Tag (m) ist ein Feiertag für ihn. 5. Gehört _____ Wagen (m) Ihnen? 6. Fragen Sie _____ Dame (f)! 7. _____ Straßenbahn (f) hält am Schillerplatz. 8. _____ Karte (f) zeigt Ihnen den Weg von hier nach Fulda. 9. _____ Haus (n) hier stammt aus dem 17. oder 18. Jahrhundert. 10. Schreiben Sie _____ Adresse (f) auf ein Stück Papier! 11. _____ Buch (n) _____ ist ein Bibliotheksbuch. 12. Sie sieht in _____ Kleid (n) sehr gut aus. 13. Wir haben, glaube ich, _____ Burg (f) am Rhein photographiert. 14. Bringen Sie bitte _____ Koffer (m) _____ auf mein Zimmer! 15. Ich habe viel von _____ Hotel (n) gehört; es soll sehr gut sein. 16. Kennen Sie _____ Stadt (f) gut? 17. In _____ Wagen (m) ist er gekommen? 18. In _____ Haus (n) wurde Mozart geboren? 19. Das können Sie in _____ Papierhandlung (f) kaufen. 20. Hat _____ Zimmer (n) elektrisches Licht? 21. Rufen Sie _____ Kellner (m)! 22. Haben Sie _____ Kellner (m) ein gutes Trinkgeld gegeben? 23. An welchem Ende _____ Korridors

(m) ist mein Zimmer? 24. In _____ Hotel (n) wohnt er? 25. _____ Schloß (n) haben Sie auf Ihrer Deutschlandreise besucht? 26. Kennen Sie _____ Jungen (m)? 27. Sie können das Dorf auf _____ Karte (f) finden. 28. _____ Rose (f) ist schön, aber _____ _____ gefällt mir besser. 29. _____ Turm (m) hier stammt aus dem Mittelalter, aber _____ _____ ist eine moderne Rekonstruktion. 30. Er hat das Autogramm von _____ Filmschauspielerin (f) in Hollywood. 31. Können Sie _____ Satz (m) verstehen? 32. Mit _____ Opernglas (n) können Sie das sehen. 33. Wissen Sie den Namen _____ Straße (f)? 34. Sprechen Sie mal mit dem Besitzer _____ Hauses (n)! 35. Der Wind kommt von _____ See (f). 36. Sie dürfen Ihr Auto vor _____ Haus (n) parken. 37. Ich kann das nicht von _____ Mann (m) erwarten. 38. Sie können das in _____ Herrengeschäft (n) kaufen. 39. Kann ich mit _____ Zug (m) von hier nach Lübeck fahren? 40. Soll ich _____ Koffer (m) packen?

E.2 *Insert the proper forms of as many of the following der-words as the meanings of the sentences permit:* **der, dieser, solcher, welcher, alle, der da:**

1. Wie heißen _____ Herren? 2. Bringen Sie bitte *den* Koffer *da* auf mein Zimmer! 3. _____ Damen sind neu hier. 4. *welche* Dichter kennen Sie? 5. Haben Sie _____ Burgen selber photographiert? 6. _____ Türme stammen aus dem Mittelalter. 7. Können Sie _____ Sätze gut verstehen? 8. Er hat _____ Kellnern ein gutes Trinkgeld gegeben. 9. Ist in _____ Zimmern elektrisches Licht? 10. Schreiben Sie _____ Adressen in Ihr Büchlein? 11. Er kennt die Namen _____ Straßen. 12. _____ Geschäfte sind von 9–12 und von 3–6 geöffnet. 13. Sie können _____ Experimente noch heute machen. 14. Kennen Sie _____ Jungen _____? 15. Sie können vor _____ Häusern parken. 16. Mit _____ Leuten kann ich gut arbeiten. 17. _____ Tiere gibt es nicht. 18. Kennen Sie _____ Studenten? 19. Man liest viel von _____ Filmen. 20. Auf _____ Autobahnen fährt es sich leicht.

E.3 *Insert from the following list a suitable adjective in its proper form:* **klein, neu, kalt, italienisch, weltberühmt, deutsch, schön, blau, gut, französisch, hübsch, hoch, frisch, grün:**

1. Geben Sie mir *kaltes* Wasser! 2. Ich möchte lieber *____* Salat. 3. Geben Sie mir ein Dutzend *frische* Eier! 4. Möchten Sie *deutsches* Schwarzbrot? 5. *deutsche* Physiker sind Röntgen, Planck, Einstein. 6. Schreiben Sie *neue* Adressen in Ihr Büchlein! 7. Kennen Sie einige Werke *guter* Dichter? 8. Er hilft _____ Studenten mit ihrem Deutsch.

9. Sie brauchen _____ Luft und Sonne. 10. Er hat _____ Augen.
11. Geben Sie mir ein Dutzend _____ Rosen! 12. Im Bus saßen nur
_____ und _____ Studenten. 13. Eine Vase mit _____ _____ Rosen
stand auf jedem Tisch. 14. Lotte hat _____ _____ Augen. 15. Die
Grimmsche Sammlung _____ Märchen ist in der ganzen Welt bekannt.
16. Hier ist eine Liste _____ und _____ Weine. 17. Die Schweiz ist ein
Land _____ Berge und _____ Seen. 18. Trinken Sie lieber _____
Milch? 19. In _____ Zimmern kann ich nicht arbeiten. 20. _____
Koffer dürfen Sie ins Flugzeug mitnehmen.

E.4 *Express the following sentences in German, using the vocabulary given
below:*

1. In which hotel is he? —In that one. 2. Is Franz in the hotel? —No,
he is in the theater. 3. Carry those suitcases over there to the hotel.
4. Give me this can and that one. 5. Goethe and Schiller are classical
writers; the former is more popular with the educated classes, the latter
with the people. 6. Those are symptoms of advanced age. 7. I love the
smell of burning wood. 8. This is my husband and those are our sons.
9. At the beginning of May we'll visit Europe. 10. You can buy these
cards at 50 pfennigs a piece.

7) Ich liebe den Geruch brennenden Holzes

VOCABULARY:

1. *the hotel*—das Hotel. 2. *the theater*—das Theater. 3. *carry*—bringen;
the suitcase—der Koffer; *the car*—das Auto. 4. *the can*—die Dose.
5. *classical writers*—Klassiker; *with the people*—beim Volk; *with educated
classes*—bei den Gebildeten; *popular*—beliebt. 6. *symptoms*—Symptome;
advanced—vorgerückt; *the age*—das Alter. 7. *the smell*—der Geruch;
burning—brennend; *the wood*—das Holz. 8. *my husband*—mein Mann;
our sons—unsere Söhne. 9. *May*—Mai. 10. *the postcard*—die Postkarte.

5. Ein-Words

ein, eine, ein	*a*	ihr, ihre, ihr	*her*
so ein, solch ein	*such a*	sein, seine, sein	*its*
kein, keine, kein	*no, not any*	unser, unsere, unser	*our*
mein, meine, mein	*my*	euer, euere, euer	*your*
dein, deine, dein	*your*	ihr, ihre, ihr	*their*
sein, seine, sein	*his*	Ihr, Ihre, Ihr	*your*

6. Declension of Ein-Words

SINGULAR

	MASCULINE	FEMININE	NEUTER
NOM.	(ein) mein Bruder	(eine) meine Schwester	(ein) unser Haus
GEN.	(eines) meines Bruders	(einer) meiner Schwester	(eines) unseres Hauses
DAT.	(einem) meinem Bruder	(einer) meiner Schwester	(einem) unserem Haus(e)
ACC.	(einen) meinen Bruder	(eine) meine Schwester	(ein) unser Haus

PLURAL, ALL GENDERS

NOM.	(keine) Ihre Freunde
GEN.	(keiner) Ihrer Freunde
DAT.	(keinen) Ihren Freunden
ACC.	(keine) Ihre Freunde

7. Ein-Words as Pronouns

a. Das ist **mein Wagen.**   *That is my car.*
   Das ist **meiner.**   *That is mine.*

   Ich habe **mein Auto** hier, aber wo ist **seins?**
   I have my car here, but where is his?

   When an **ein**-word is used without a noun, that is, when it functions as
   a pronoun, it takes the ending of the **der**-word.

b. Seine Reise war interessanter als **meine / die meine / die meinige.**
   His trip was more interesting than mine.

   The two additional forms for the possessive pronoun (**die meine, die
   meinige**) are normally not used in conversation.

8. Variations in the Use of the Indefinite Article

Er ist **Zahnarzt.**   *He is a dentist.*
Er ist **ein guter Zahnarzt.**   *He is a good dentist.*

Sie ist **Amerikanerin.**   *She is an American.*
Sie ist **eine junge Amerikanerin.**   *She is a young American woman.*

The indefinite article is omitted when a predicate noun signifies a profession, nationality, condition, and the like. If, however, the noun is modified, it requires the indefinite article.

Exercises

E.5 *Insert suitable ein-words from the following list. Choose as many as the meanings of the sentences permit:* **ein, so ein, kein, was für ein, mein, dein, sein, ihr** (*her*), **unser, euer, ihr** (*their*), **Ihr** (*your*):

1. Ich habe _____ Freund in Amerika. 2. Ich habe _____ Schwester in den Staaten. 3. Er besitzt _____ Hotel in USA. 4. Hübsch wohnen Sie hier in _____ Sommerhäuschen. 5. Hübsch wohnst du hier in _____ Sommerhäuschen. 6. Hübsch wohnt ihr hier in _____ Sommerhäuschen. 7. Hübsch wohnen sie hier in _____ Sommerhäuschen. 8. Er wohnt sehr schön in _____ neuen Sommerhäuschen. 9. Sie fühlt sich wohl in _____ neuen Sommerhäuschen. 10. Er saß den ganzen Abend auf dem Sofa und sagte _____ Wort. 11. Wir Geschwister haben _____ Eltern nie vergessen. 12. Seine Eltern glauben, _____ Sohn ist ein Genie. 13. Die Kinder hatten _____ Vater früh verloren. 14. Man fand die Papiere im Büro _____ Firma, für die er lange gearbeitet hatte. 15. Was für _____ Mann! 16. Was für _____ Sekretärin ist sie? 17. Für _____ Frau ist das Beste nicht gut genug. 18. _____ Kindern gebe ich nur die beste Milch. 19. Für _____ Vater haben wir Kinder immer gerne gearbeitet. 20. Für _____ Eltern haben wir Kinder immer gerne gearbeitet. 21. Für _____ Chef hat er immer gerne gearbeitet. 22. Was hat Heidi _____ Mann zum Geburtstag geschenkt? 23. Was hat Peter _____ Frau zu Weihnachten geschenkt? 24. Was sollen wir _____ Kindern zu Weihnachten schenken? 25. Das ist ein Geschenk _____ Kinder. 26. Geben Sie mir bitte die Adresse _____ Hotels! 27. Haben Sie die neue Adresse _____ Büros bei sich? 28. War dies das Hotel _____ Vaters, Max? 29. Sagt mal, Kinder, wo sind _____ Eltern?

E.6 *Insert suitable ein-words as pronouns:*

1. Ist das sein Wagen? Nein, das ist _____. 2. Hier ist der Mantel Ihrer Frau, aber wo ist _____, Herr Doktor? 3. Hier ist _____ Eintrittskarte, Fräulein Hertes, und hier ist _____, Anna. 4. Hat er Kinder? Nein, er hat _____. 5. Sein Auto ist größer als _____.

E.7 *Decide whether to use the indefinite article with the words in parentheses:*

EXAMPLE: (Lehrer) Mein Freund will _____ werden.
　　　　　　Mein Freund will Lehrer werden.

1. (Flieger) Mein Bruder will _____ werden. 2. (guter Flieger) Ich bin

sicher, er wird _____ werden.   3. (junger Deutscher) Unser Lehrer ist
_____.   4. (Patient) Sie sind noch _____ und müssen Ihrem Doktor
gehorchen.   5. (Engländerin) Sind Sie _____?   6. (junge Engländerin)
Sie ist _____.   7. (Demokrat oder Republikaner) Sind die beiden _____?
8. (Republikaner, Demokrat) Der eine ist _____ und der andere _____.
9. (Hausfrau) Sind Sie _____?   10. (gute Hausfrau) Ich weiß, Sie sind
_____.

9. Adjectives without Endings

a. Predicate Adjectives

Der Tee ist / wird **kalt.**	*The tea is / is getting cold.*
Die Suppe ist / wird **kalt.**	*The soup is / is getting cold.*
Das Essen ist **gut** aber **teuer.**	*The food is good but expensive.*

Adjectives used with **sein** (*to be*) or **werden** (*to become, get*) are called
predicative adjectives. Such adjectives have no endings.

b. Adverbs

Hier müssen Sie **langsam** fahren.	*You must drive slowly here.*
Sie versteht mich **gut.**	*She understands me well.*

An adjective modifying a verb is called an adverb. German adverbs have
no endings.

10. Adjectives with Endings

a. Unpreceded Adjectives

NOMINATIVE SINGULAR

MASCULINE	FEMININE	NEUTER
deutsch**er** Schinken	deutsch**e** Wurst	deutsch**es** Bier
gut**er** deutsch**er** Schinken	gut**e** deutsche Wurst	gut**es** deutsches Bier

As shown in Section 2, adjectives preceding a noun as its only modifiers
have the endings of **der**-words. It does not matter whether one or several
adjectives precede the noun.

b. Numerical Adjectives

Adjectives such as **deutsch, gut, schön** attribute a quality to a noun and are called attributive adjectives. Another group of adjectives deals only with quantity. They are called numerical adjectives:

alle	*all*	**manche**	*many*
andere	*other*	**mehrere**	*several*
beide	*both*	**viele**	*many*
einige	*a few, some*	**wenige**	*few*
etliche	*some*		

DECLENSION

NOM.	einige Bücher
GEN.	einiger Bücher
DAT.	einigen Büchern
ACC.	einige Bücher

A descriptive adjective takes the same ending as the numerical adjective, except after **alle, beide,** and **manche,** when it takes **-en** in the four cases:

NOM.	viele neue Bücher	alle neuen Bücher
GEN.	vieler neuer Bücher	aller neuen Bücher
DAT.	vielen neuen Büchern	allen neuen Büchern
ACC.	viele neue Bücher	alle neuen Bücher

c. Adjectives preceded by the definite article or a **der**-word

SINGULAR

	MASCULINE	FEMININE	NEUTER
NOM.	der alte Herr	die alte Dame	das alte Hotel
	dieser alte Herr	diese alte Dame	dieses alte Hotel
ACC.		die alte Dame	das alte Hotel
		diese alte Dame	dieses alte Hotel

An adjective preceded by the definite article or a **der**-word ends in **-e** in all nominative forms and in the feminine and neuter of the accusative. In all other cases an adjective preceded by a definite article or a **der**-word ends in **-en**:

Er kennt **den alten** Herrn. Er kennt **diesen alten** Herrn.
die Familie **des alten** Herrn
die Familie **dieser alten** Dame
in **allen alten** Hotels

Observe:

Es ist **derselbe** Herr, **dieselbe** Dame.

Derselbe (*the same*) is declined as if **selb-** were an ordinary adjective.

d. Adjectives preceded by the indefinite article or an **ein**-word

To understand adjective endings after an **ein**-word, it is useful to realize that the German ear demands some indication of case and gender in the words modifying a noun. **Der**-words and unpreceded adjectives do that:

> **der** Schinken, **dieser** Schinken
> **die** Wurst, **frische** Wurst
> **das** Mineralwasser, **deutsches** Mineralwasser

The feminine form of **ein**-words does that, too:

> **eine** Mutter, **meine** Mutter

However, **ein, mein,** etc. may be followed by either a masculine noun (**Vater**) or a neuter noun (**Kind**). Since the **ein**-word does not indicate the gender here, an adjective preceded by such an ambiguous **ein**-word must bear the gender indication:

> mein **lieber** Vater, mein **liebes** Kind.

Observe the following table:

	SINGULAR		
	MASCULINE	FEMININE	NEUTER
NOM.	**ein alter** Vater **mein** etc.	**eine alte** Mutter **meine** etc.	**ein liebes** Kind **mein** etc.
ACC.	**einen alten** Vater **meinen** etc.	**eine alte** Mutter **meine** etc.	**ein liebes** Kind **mein** etc.

Examples for remaining cases:

GEN. SING. (three genders) — der Besitzer **eines neuen** Wagens / **einer neuen** Farm / **eines neuen** Hotels

DAT. SING. (three genders) — in **meinem neuen** Wagen / auf **seiner neuen** Farm / in **einem neuen** Hotel

PLURAL (in all cases) — **keine neuen** Hotels
das Problem **aller alten** Patienten
mit **seinen neuen** Studenten
ihre blauen Augen

11. Summary of Adjective Endings

Adjective endings after articles and **ein-** or **der-**words follow these patterns:

der -e Herr	ein -er Herr
die -e Dame	eine -e Dame
das -e Kind	ein -es Kind
All other forms: **-en**	

Observe:

> **edel:** eine **edle** Tat
> **unser:** in **unsrem** Hause

Adjectives ending in **-el** or **-er** usually drop the **e** when inflected, especially in spoken German.

12. Adjectives Used as Nouns

German, more than English, uses adjectives as nouns, including present and past participles functioning as adjectives. Such nouns retain the adjective declension. They are, of course, capitalized.

EXAMPLES:

der Arme *the poor man*	**die Arme** *the poor woman*	**die Armen** *the poor*
ein Armer	**eine Arme**	**Arme**
der Deutsche	**die Deutsche**	**die Deutschen**
ein Deutscher	**eine Deutsche**	**Deutsche**

Common nouns of this type:

der Angestellte *employee*	**der Kranke** *sick person*
der Anwesende *person present*	**der Reiche** *rich man*
der Arbeitslose *unemployed man*	**der Reisende** *traveler*
der Beamte *official;* but **die Beamtin**	**der Verwandte** *relative*
der Bekannte *acquaintance*	**das Böse** *evil*
der Erwachsene *adult*	**das Neue** *the new* (*thing*)
der Fremde *stranger*	**das Interessanteste** *the most interesting thing*

Exercises

E.8 *Substitute for the definite article the words in parentheses and add the correct ending to the adjective (Be careful. The dash may not indicate a missing ending.):*

1. Der Autor heißt Gerhart Hauptmann (dies—, dies— deutsch—).
2. Der Mechaniker kann das reparieren (jed—, kein—, jed— geschickt—, ein geschickt—). 3. Wo ist der Kellner (unser—, dein—, unser alt—)?
4. Der Doktor ist hier (unser—, Ihr—, mein—, welch—, ein—, ein deutsch—). 5. Der Milchmann kommt (unser—, Ihr—). 6. Wer ist der Herr (dies—, dies— jung—)? 7. Der Krieg dauerte 30 Jahre (welch—, dies— furchtbar—). 8. Der Dampfer fährt in einer halben Stunde (unser—, ein ander—). 9. Der Bruder ist Kaufmann (mein—, mein— jünger—, unser—, unser ältest—). 10. Der Zug ist noch nicht hier (dein—, dies—). 11. Der Wagen ist in der Garage (Ihr—, mein neu—, unser alt—). 12. Der Freund (mein—, mein lieb—). 13. Der Schinken kostet drei Mark das Pfund (gekocht—, jed— westfälisch—). 14. Der Kaffee ist zu stark für mich (dies—, dies— schwarz—, schwarz—).
15. Der Film ist so interessant (nicht jed—, nicht jed— amerikanisch—, kein neu—).

E.9 *Substitute for the definite article the words in parentheses and add the correct ending to the adjective:*

1. Die Milch ist gut (dies—, unser—, mein— frisch—). 2. Die Suppe ist gut für Sie (dies—, heiß—, dies— heiß—). 3. Die Bank ist heute geschlossen (jed—, unser—, kein—, die deutsch—). 4. Die Frau ist zu schwach für so eine Arbeit (Ihr—, mein—, kein—, dies— alt—). 5. Die Adresse steht nicht im Telephonbuch (dies—, ihr—, sein—, sein— neu—).
6. Die Kirche ist sehr alt (dies—, unser—, unser— schön—). 7. Das Klima ist gut für ihn (dies—, warm—, unser—, unser— warm—). 8. Die Photographie gefällt mir gut (sein—, dies—, Ihr— neu—). 9. Die Fahrkarte ist die ganze Woche gültig (jed—, dies—, mein—, kein—, dies— gelb—). 10. Die Kritik machte ihn ärgerlich (kein—, kein— scharf—, jed— scharf—). 11. Die Hand ist geschwollen (sein— link—, welch—).
12. Die Aussprache ist gut (sein—, sein— deutsch—, Ihr—). 13. Die Drogerie ist heute offen (unser—, kein—, jed—, welch—, unser— amerikanisch—). 14. Die Geschichte ist interessant (nicht jed—, sein— klein—, ein— solch—). 15. Literatur interessiert ihn nicht (die modern—, modern—, unser— modern— deutsch—). 16. Das ist die Welt (mein—, mein— klein—, unser—). 17. Die Frau ist Sängerin (sein—, sein—

jung—). 18. Die Vorlesung beginnt um drei (kein—, unser—, die nächst—, unser— nächst—). 19. Die Milch ist im Kühlschrank (frisch—, die frisch—, Ihr—). 20. Die Frau hat ihren Mann verloren (dies—, dies— jung—).

E.10 *Substitute for the definite article the words in parentheses and add the correct ending to the adjective:*

1. Das Museum ist am Montag geschlossen (jed—, dies—). 2. Das Hotel ist in der Nähe (ein—, ein nicht zu teuer—, kein—, kein gut—). 3. Das Land braucht Frieden (jed—, unser—, unser arm—). 4. Das Zimmer liegt nach der Straße (jed—, unser—, unser alt—). 5. Das Auto ist mir zu teuer (dies—, so ein—, ein neu—). 6. Das Bier ist zu stark für ihn (dies—, dies— bayrisch—, bayrisch—, unser bayrisch—). 7. Das Haus ist nicht mehr da (sein alt—, unser alt—, dies— alt—). 8. Das Messer ist nicht scharf genug (mein—, Ihr alt—). 9. Das Licht ist nicht gut zum Lesen (dies—, dies— schwach—, schwach—). 10. Das Gespräch interessierte ihn (unser lang—, dies—, dies— lang—). 11. Das Fleisch ist im Kühlschrank (gebraten—, das gebraten—). 12. Das Sprichwort sagt: Hunger ist der beste Koch (das alt—, ein alt—, dies alt—). 13. Das Brot ist gut (das deutsch—, deutsch—, unser deutsch—).

E.11 *Substitute for the definite article the words in parentheses and add the correct ending to the adjective:*

1. Die Leute verstehen ihn nicht (dies—, manch— jung—, dies— jung—). 2. Die Koffer sind im Auto (Ihr—, Ihr— beid—, die beid—, welch—, welch— beid—, all—). 3. Die Wagen sind auf dem Parkplatz (wie viel—, unser—, unser— neu—, alle neu—, viele neu—). 4. Die Eltern leben in Europa (mein—, sein—, sein— alt—). 5. Die Züge fahren nur bis München (dies—, welch—, all—). 6. Die Kinder mögen das nicht (unser—, unser— klein—, amerikanisch—, viel— klein—). 7. Die Zimmer gefallen uns (Ihr—, Ihr— beid—, dies— klein—, all—). 8. Die Läden sind heute geschlossen (viel—, viel— klein—, all— klein—, beid— klein—). 9. Die Bomben fielen auf das Stadtzentrum (viel—, viel— amerikanisch—, amerikanisch—, all— amerikanisch—). 10. Die Nächte sind kühl (die meist—, afrikanisch—, die afrikanisch—, all— afrikanisch—). 11. Die Blumen wachsen hier das ganze Jahr (wild—, die wild—, schön— wild—, viel— wild—). 12. Die Prüfungen in diesem Fach sind schwer (unser—, unser— lang—, all—). 13. Die Schwestern sind verheiratet (mein—, mein— älter—, all— älter—). 14. Die Schulen haben kürzere Sommerferien (die europäisch—, viel— europäisch—, all— europäisch—). 15. Die Studenten applaudierten (unser—, unser— jung—, all— jung—, viel— jung—).

E.12 *Using the genitive, connect the following word groups:*

EXAMPLE: der Kapitän, das deutsche Schiff
der Kapitän des deutschen Schiffes

1. die Farbe, das nördliche Meer. 2. das Problem, das geteilte Deutschland. 3. das Klima, der europäische Kontinent. 4. die Tiefe, das Meer. 5. die Schönheit, diese Landschaft. 6. die Größe, die Vereinigten Staaten. 7. die Kraft, ein indischer Elefant. 8. die Lichter, der letzte Zug. 9. das Licht, die südliche Sonne. 10. die Zukunft, die afrikanischen Staaten. 11. die Geschichte, das alte Griechenland. 12. die Geschichte, das mittelalterliche Rom. 13. das Leben, diese arme alte Frau. 14. jedes Zimmer, ein modernes Hotel. 15. die letzte Reise, der alte Dampfer. 16. das Netz, die deutschen Eisenbahnen. 17. der Charakter, diese Leute. 18. das Leben, alle jungen Menschen. 19. das Ende, unsere schönen Sommerferien. 20. die Aussprache, diese deutschlernenden Amerikaner. 21. der Geschmack, die frischen Erdbeeren. 22. das Gepäck, diese deutschen Herren. 23. die Schönheit, die mitteldeutschen Gebirge. 24. die Grenzen, alle europäischen Länder. 25. der Grund, viele europäische Kriege. 26. die Experimente, einige deutsche Wissenschaftler. 27. die Resultate, wenige wissenschaftliche Experimente. 28. das Verkehrsproblem, viele europäische Städte. 29. das Urteil, diese berühmten Gelehrten. 30. die Zeitungen, alle deutschen Großstädte.

E.13 *Supply the correct dative forms of the words in parentheses:*

EXAMPLE:

Singular: Zeigen Sie _____ das Zimmer (der Amerikaner)!
Zeigen Sie dem Amerikaner das Zimmer!

Zeigen Sie _____ das Zimmer (die Amerikanerin)!
Zeigen Sie der Amerikanerin das Zimmer!

Plural: Zeigen Sie _____ das Zimmer (die Amerikaner)!
Zeigen Sie den Amerikanern das Zimmer!

1. Geben Sie _____ ein Trinkgeld (jeder Hoteldiener)? 2. Schreiben Sie _____ Briefe (die alten Dame)? 3. Das Hotel gehört _____ (ein deutschen Konzern). 4. Erzählen Sie _____ alles, was Sie gesehen haben (unser Komitee)! 5. Sagen Sie _____ nichts davon (dem alten Herr)! 6. Sie müssen _____ Ihren Paß zeigen (dieser Leute). 7. Das Auto gehört _____ im schwarzen Mantel (die junge Dame). 8. Geben Sie bitte die Speisekarte _____ am Nachbartisch (die jungen Herren)! 9. Wie kann man das _____ erklären (ein jungen Mensch)? 10. Geben Sie Ihren Paß und diese Papiere _____ (der nächste Herr)! 11. Geben Sie _____

diese Puppe (Ihr kleines Töchterchen)! 12. Das muß ich _____ erzählen
(mein junger Freund). 13. Geben Sie _____ zwanzig Pfennig (die
Kleine)! 14. Sagen Sie _____, daß sie im Dom ihren Kopf bedecken
muß (die junge Dame)! 15. Helfen Sie _____ (der Blinde)!

E.14 *Supply the correct accusative forms of the words in parentheses:*

1. Wir kennen _den_ nicht (der junge Herr). 2. Beschreiben Sie _den_
(der alte Mann)! 3. Fahren Sie _____ (dieser alte Wagen)? 4. Fragen
Sie _____ (der nächste Schutzmann)! 5. Zeigen Sie uns _____ (Ihr
amerikanischer Paß)! 6. Geben Sie mir _____ (dies kleine Päckchen)!
7. Heute haben wir Fleisch, Kartoffeln und _____ (grüner Salat).
8. Geben Sie mir _____ Butter (ein halbes Pfund)! 9. Geben Sie mir
ein Pfund _____ (gekochter Schinken)! 10. Kauf mir ein Dutzend
_____ (italienischen Apfelsinen)! 11. Verkaufen Sie hier _____
(deutsches Schwarzbrot)? 12. Ich muß _____ verkaufen (mein alter
Wagen). 13. Warum kaufen Sie sich _____ (ein neuer Volkswagen)?
14. Ich möchte _____ in Hamburg besuchen (meine deutschen Verwandten). 15. Wenn Sie nur New York und Washington kennen, können Sie nicht sagen, daß Sie _____ kennen (die Vereinigten Staaten).
16. Bringen Sie _____ mit (Ihr neuer Freund)! 17. Bringen Sie uns
drei Tassen Kaffee, aber _____ bitte (heißer Kaffee)! 18. Sie liebt
_____ (ein deutscher Student). 19. Ich habe _____ in der Tasche
(kein Pfennig). 20. Bei diesem Wetter sollten Sie _____ tragen (ein
wärmerer Mantel). 21. Er liebt _____ Italiens (die warme Sonne).
22. Kennen Sie _____ (der schöne bayrische Wald)? 23. Geben Sie
dem Herrn _____ nach dem Hof (ein ruhiges Zimmer)! 24. Er beschrieb uns (das bayrische Volksfest). 25. Bringen Sie _____ mit (Ihre
netten jungen Freunde)! 26. Erzählen Sie auch uns _____ (diese lustigen
Geschichten)! 27. Geben Sie uns _____ für Ihre Tat (ein Grund)!
28. Ich mag _____ (kein fettes Fleisch). 29. Geben Sie mir bitte nur
_____ (ein kleines Stück)!

E.15 *Read the following sentences aloud to train your ear for the common* **-en**
ending:

1. Die heiß— Tage und die kalt— Nächte machten ihn krank. 2. Er ist
Besitzer eines modern— Hotels. 3. In jedem arm— Lande finden Sie
alle modern— Probleme. 4. Mögen Sie die Farbe meines neu— Autos?
5. Sie zeigte dem italienisch— Beamten ihren amerikanisch— Paß.
6. Ich möchte die beid— Zimmer am ander— Ende des Korridors.
7. Als Besitzer einer groß— Fabrik kann er sich solche lang— Reisen
erlauben. 8. Er spricht mit jedem hübsch— Mädchen. 9. Lindberg flog

in seinem klein— Flugzeug über den Atlantisch— Ozean. 10. Lesen Sie nur die deutsch— Zeitungen? 11. Welche englisch— Kriegsschiffe sind jetzt an der norwegisch— Küste? 12. Kennen Sie den jung— Journalisten, der diese miserabl— Artikel geschrieben hat? 13. Der große Gelehrte starb in seinem klein—, kalt— Hotelzimmer. 14. Auf diesem Bilde sehen Sie den Präsidenten der Vereinigt— Staaten vor einem amerikanisch— Flugzeug auf seiner letzt— Reise nach Europa. 15. Ich brauche einen neu— Koffer.

E.16 *Supply the missing endings. The gender of nouns used in the singular is indicated:*

1. Was für eine Delikatesse! Westfälisch—r Schinken (m) mit süß—en Butter (f) auf deutsch—r Schwarzbrot (n). 2. Der arm— Student (m) fuhr in seinem billig— Auto (n) vom sonnig— Kalifornien (n) bis zum kalt—s Alaska (n). 3. Wie heißt die nett—en Frau (f) da mit den drei hübsch— Kindern? 4. Sie hat schön— blau— Augen und lang— blond—es Haar (n). 5. Mozarts Vater machte mit seinem klein—en Jungen (m) und seiner klein— Tochter (f) eine lang—en Konzertreise (f) durch Europa. 6. Haben Sie vielleicht auch ein— reich— alt— Onkel (m) in den Vereinigt—en Staaten? 7. Das war das richtig— Wort (n) zur richtig— Zeit (f). 8. In der nächst— Stadt (f) kaufen wir deutsch— Delikatessen. 9. Westfälisch— Schinken (m) ist in der ganz— Welt (f) berühmt. 10. Trinken Sie dunkl— oder hell— Bier (n)? Weder das ein— noch das andr—. Bringen Sie mir bitte frisch— Milch (f)!

13. Comparison of Adjectives

a. Formation and Use

POSITIVE	COMPARATIVE	SUPERLATIVE
schön	schöner	am schönsten / der schönste
interessant	interessanter	am interessantesten / der interessanteste

1. German forms the comparison of all adjectives by adding **-er** and the superlative by adding **-st**. Adjectives ending in **d, t, s, ß, tz, z** add **-est** for the superlative.

2. When preceding the noun, superlatives of adjectives have the form **der, die, das —(e)ste**:

Das schnellste Pferd im Steeplechase war Attila.
The fastest horse in the steeplechase was Attila.

3. The superlative form **am —(e)sten** is used for a predicate adjective:

Attila läuft **am schnellsten,** wenn er Konkurrenz hat.
Attila runs fastest if he has competition.

4. There are two ways of expressing comparison:

Er ist **so alt wie** ich.   *He is as old as I.*
Er ist **älter als** ich.   *He is older than I.*

b. Formation for Adjectives of One Syllable

POSITIVE	COMPARATIVE	SUPERLATIVE
kalt	kälter	am kältesten / der kälteste
jung	jünger	am jüngsten / der jüngste
kurz	kürzer	am kürzesten / der kürzeste
alt	älter	am ältesten / der älteste

Adjectives of one syllable usually modify the vowels **a, o, u** (not **au**) in the comparative and superlative. Common exceptions are: **falsch, froh, klar, rund, voll, wahr.**

c. Adjectives with Irregular Comparatives and Superlatives

POSITIVE	COMPARATIVE	SUPERLATIVE
groß	größer	am größten / der größte
hoch	höher	am höchsten / der höchste
nahe	näher	am nächsten / der nächste
gut	besser	am besten / der beste
viel	mehr[1]	am meisten / der meiste
wenig	weniger[1]	am wenigsten / der wenigste

d. Special Meanings of Adjectives in the Comparative

der **ältere** Herr   *the elderly gentleman*
ein **längerer** Aufenthalt   *a prolonged stay*
neuere Sprachen / Geschichte   *modern languages / history*

14. Comparison of Adverbs

a. Formation

Adverbs have the same comparison as predicate adjectives. A few adverbs, however, have irregular comparatives and superlatives:

[1] is not declined

POSITIVE	COMPARATIVE	SUPERLATIVE
gern	lieber	am liebsten
gut / wohl	besser	am besten
viel	mehr	am meisten

EXAMPLES:

„Sie trinken Bier **gern,** nicht wahr, Herr Höffner?“
„Ja, Frau Schulz, aber Wein trinke ich **lieber,**“
„Und ich trinke Milch **am liebsten!**“

b. Special Meanings of Adverbs in the Superlative

erstens	*in the first place*
spätestens	*at the latest*
höchstens	*at the most*
wenigstens	*at least*
meistens	*mostly*

Exercises

E.17 *Insert the adjective in the comparative or superlative form:*

1. (billig) In USA ist die Milch _____ als in Europa.   2. (interessant)
Für viele ist das alte Europa _____ als das moderne.   3. (interessant)
Die _____ Frau der Antike war Kleopatra.   4. (wild) Die _____ Großkatze ist der Leopard.   5. (heiß) Der _____ Sommer in Karlsruhe war
der vergangene.   6. (hoch) Das Empire State Gebäude ist _____ als der
Kölner Dom.   7. (viel) Die Kritiker haben viel über Hemingways Jugend-
werke geschrieben, aber _____ über seine späteren Werke.   8. (gern)
Spielen Sie gern Tischtennis? —Nein, ich spiele _____ Tennis. —Und was
spielen Sie am _____?   9. (kalt) Es wird immer _____.   10. (kalt) Wie
kalt war es am _____ Tag?   11. (jung) Barbara ist _____ als Linda, und
Lisa ist mein _____ Kind.   12. (kurz) Das lateinische Wort *i!* (geh!) ist
das _____ Wort der lateinischen Sprache.   13. (groß) Der russische Bär
ist groß, der amerikanische Grislybär ist aber noch _____, und der
_____ Bär der Welt ist der Riesenbär von Alaska.   14. (hoch) Ist der
Watzmann der _____ Berg Deutschlands? —Nein, die Zugspitze ist
_____.   15. (viel) Fünfzehn Prozent! Das ist zu viel für ein Trinkgeld.
—Nicht in diesem Restaurant. Hier müssen Sie _____ geben.   16. (viel)
Ich habe viele Bücher aus der Bibliothek geholt, aber die _____ habe ich
nicht gebrauchen können.   17. (spät) Sie müssen den Artikel _____ am
20. März beendet haben.   18. (wenig) Hat er sich _____ entschuldigt?

19. (hoch) Die Reparatur Ihres Autos wird *höchstens* eine Stunde dauern.
20. (gut) Es geht ihm noch nicht gut, aber es geht ihm schon *besser*.
21. (gut) Das *Beste* wäre, wenn Sie zu einem Arzt gingen. 22. (viel)
Wir alle freuen uns auf Ihr Kommen, aber die Kinder am *meisten*. 23. (alt)
Er ist ein *älter* Herr mit etwas Grau in den Haaren. 24. (gut) Ist dies
wirklich die *beste* Waschmaschine. 25. (viel) Kühe geben die *mehr*
Milch, wenn sie Radiomusik hören. 26. (viel) Jetzt ist es aber genug,
oder wollen Sie noch *mehr*.

15. Gender of Nouns

Der Bäcker (*the baker*) is masculine because a profession is represented in
German as in English by a male. **Die Kuh** is female because of its natural
gender. **Die Zeitung** is feminine because all nouns ending in **-ung** are feminine in German. The gender of a vast majority of German nouns depends
on their meaning or their ending. It is therefore possible to determine the
gender of many nouns with the help of the following rules.

16. Gender According to Meaning

a. Masculines

1. Male beings:

   der Mann, der Sohn, der Onkel, der Löwe, der Stier, der Hahn, der Junge,
   etc.

2. Nouns denoting a profession, occupation, activity, nationality, or
   membership in a political party with which we normally associate a
   man:

   **der Arzt, der Koch, der Fischer, der Arbeiter, der General, der Soldat, der
   Schwimmer, der Deutsche, der Russe, der Demokrat, der Kommunist**

3. The seasons, months, days, and time divisions of the day:

   **der Frühling, der Sommer, der Januar, der Februar, der Sonntag, der Montag,
   der Morgen, der Mittag,** etc.

   Exception: **die Nacht**

4. Weather phenomena, stones, directions of the compass. Within these
   categories, some word groups consist entirely of masculine nouns.
   Such groupings do not represent grammatical rules in the narrower
   sense of the word, but a memory help:

Winds: **der Wind, der Sturm, der Orkan, der Taifun, der Zephyr**
Weather: **der Regen, der Sonnenschein, der Blitz, der Donner, der Hagel, der Schnee, der Nebel, der Frost**

Exceptions: **das Wetter, das Gewitter**

Stones: **der Stein, der Sandstein, der Quarz, der Granit, der Diamant, der Rubin, der Felsen**

Directions: **der Norden, der Süden, der Westen, der Osten**

b. Feminines

1. Female beings:

die Frau, die Tochter, die Schwester, die Tante; die Kuh, die Henne

There are only three exceptions: **das Mädchen** and **das Fräulein** are neuter nouns because of their grammatical forms **-chen** and **-lein** (see 17, c, 1); **das Weib,** meaning *woman* in a poetic, medical, or derogatory sense.

2. Most German rivers:

die Donau, die Elbe, die Lahn, die Oder, die Ruhr, die Weser, etc.

Remember as exceptions: **der Rhein, der Main, der Neckar**

3. Numbers:

die Null, die Eins, die Zwei, die Zehn

Exceptions: **das Einmaleins, das Hundert, das Tausend**

4. Names of ships:

die Bremen, die Europa, die United States, die Normandie, die Washington

5. Names of cigars and cigarettes, because **Zigarre** and **Zigarette** are feminine:

die Havanna, die Virginia, die Finas, die Eckstein

c. Neuters

1. Names of continents, countries, provinces, states, islands, and cities:

(das) **Afrika,** (das) **Europa,** (das) **Deutschland,** (das) **England,** (das) **Bayern,** (das) **Iowa,** (das) **Helgoland,** (das) **Berlin,** (das) **Chicago**

Note: Nouns belonging to this category do not use the article unless they are modified:

das Hamburg der Vorkriegszeit, das Korsika Napoleons, das alte Europa, das neue Deutschland

Exceptions: Feminine are **die Normandie, die Tschechoslowakei, die Türkei, die Mongolei, die Schweiz**

2. Metals and chemical elements:

das Blech, das Blei, das Eisen, das Gold, das Kupfer, das Silber; das Chlor, das Helium, das Natrium, das Wolfram

3. Colors:

das berühmte Rot Tizians, das Blau des Himmels, das erste Grün des Frühlings

4. Letters of the alphabet:

das ABC; Das deutsche w wird beinahe wie **das englische v** ausgesprochen.

5. Adverbs, phrases, and sentences:

Er denkt nur an **das Heute; das Morgen** kümmert ihn nicht.
Das berühmte „Einmal ist keinmal" ist nur eine Halbwahrheit.
Das scharfe „Sie sind jetzt an der Reihe" erschreckte ihn.

17. Gender According to Form

a. Masculines

1. Nouns ending in **-er, -or, -eur** signify a profession or a male being:

der Arbeiter, der Schuhmacher, der Schwimmer; der Doktor, der Professor, der Inspektor; der Friseur

Some nouns ending in **-or** denote a thing acting as an agent: **der Motor.**

2. Most monosyllabic nouns derived from a verbal stem form:

kaufen: der Kauf; fallen: der Fall; schießen: der Schuß; schließen: der Schluß; beißen: der Biß; reißen: der Riß

3. Words of non-German origin ending in **-ismus** and **-us:**

der Realismus, der Kommunismus, der Bazillus, der Typhus

b. Feminines

1. Nouns ending in **-in,** representing the feminine counterparts of words mentioned in 16, a, 2:

die Ärztin, die Arbeiterin, die Lehrerin, die Verkäuferin, die Opernsängerin

2. Nouns ending in **-heit, -keit, -schaft**:

die Schönheit, die Tapferkeit, die Freundschaft

3. Nouns ending in **-e**:

die Rose, die Farbe, die Hilfe, etc.

Exceptions: Words that are masculine by gender:

> **der Russe, der Riese, der Kunde, der Löwe, der Junge, der Neffe** (see 16, a, 1)

> Abstract nouns formed from adjectives:

> **das Gute, das Schöne, das Wahre**

> Nouns beginning with **Ge-**:

> **das Gebirge, das Gebäude**

> Other exceptions:

> **das Ende, das Interesse, das Knie, das Auge, das Café; der Friede, der Gedanke, der Kaffee, der Käse, der Name, der See, der Tee**

4. Nouns ending in **-ei** and **-ung**:

die Bäckerei, die Fleischerei, die Hoffnung, die Zeitung

5. Nouns ending in **-ion**; note the stress on the last syllable:

die Nation, die Religion, die Organisation

6. Nouns ending in **-ie** with English equivalents in *y*. Note that in German the stress is always on the last syllable:

die Philosophie, die Theorie, die Zoologie

c. Neuters

1. Nouns ending in **-chen** and **-lein**. These two diminutive suffixes make every noun neuter, regardless of the gender of the noun to which they are attached. This explains why **Mädchen** and **Fräulein** are neuter nouns:

der Hund	**das Hündchen**	**das Hündlein**
die Katze	**das Kätzchen**	**das Kätzlein**

2. Nouns formed from infinitives: **das Rauchen, das Schwimmen, das Singen.** Such verbal nouns are expressed in English by the gerund (*the singing*).

3. Nouns beginning with **Ge-: das Gefühl, das Gesicht;** many of these Ge-compounds end in **-e: das Gebäude, das Gebirge.**

Exceptions:

der Gesang, die Gefahr, die Gewalt, die Geschichte

Note that words like **Gelegenheit** and **Gesellschaft** are feminine because of their suffixes **-heit** and **-schaft** (see 17, b, 2).

18. Gender of Compound Nouns

Observe:

die Universität—das Buch—der Laden: der Universitätsbuchladen

The gender of the last noun determines the gender of a compound noun.

19. Nouns with Two Genders

der Band, ⸚e	volume	das Band, ⸚er	ribbon
der Erbe, -n, -n	heir	das Erbe	inheritance
der Gehalt, -e	content	das Gehalt, ⸚er	salary
der Heide, -n, -n	heathen	die Heide, -n	heath, heather
der Hut, ⸚e	hat	die Hut	guard
der Kunde, -n, -n	customer	die Kunde, -n	news
der Leiter, -	manager	die Leiter, -n	ladder
der Schild, -e	shield	das Schild, -er	signboard, label
der See, -n	lake	die See, -n	sea
das Steuer, -	rudder, helm	die Steuer, -n	tax
der Tau	dew	das Tau, -e	rope
der Tor, -en, -en	fool	das Tor, -e	gate
der Verdienst, -e	earnings	das Verdienst, -e	merit

Exercises

E.18 *Insert the definite or indefinite article, an ein-word or der-word required by the meaning of the sentence. Omit it if it should not be used. The blank in such a case is used only to test you:*

1. _____ Stier verwundete _____ Stierkämpfer durch _____ Hornstoß.
2. _der_ Name _der_ Matadors steht auf dem Programm. 3. _____ Papst zeigte sich an einem Fenster des Vatikans. 4. _____ Eskimo

kämpfte mit _____ Eisbären. 5. _____ Violinvirtuose Paganini spielte
wie _____ Dämon, sagte _____ Publikum _____ frühen 19. Jahrhun-
derts. 6. _____ Tulpe wird in Holland kultiviert. 7. _____ Beate
Fernandi war _____ Verkäuferin in einem Handschuhgeschäft, bevor sie
_____ Filmschauspielerin wurde. 8. Kennen Sie den Namen _____
deutschen Filmschauspielers? 9. _____ Stärke _____ Gladiators war
_____ Schutz gegen _____ Schnelligkeit _____ leichteren Spartakus.
10. Der Leser eines neuen Buches sagte einmal zu _____ Kritiker Lessing:
In diesem Buch steht vieles, was gut und neu ist. „Ja", antwortete Lessing,
„aber _____ Gute ist nicht neu und _____ Neue ist nicht gut."
11. _____ Mädchen zeigte _____ Freundin _____ glitzernden Diamanten. _____ Freundin sagte: Solch _____ Freund möchte ich auch haben.
12. Ohne _____ Sekretärin könnte ich nicht viel tun. 13. _____ Arzt
gab _____ Patienten _____ Serum gegen _____ Biß _____ Schlange.
14. _____ Schuß, _____ Schrei, und alles war wieder still. 15. _____
Major kam von _____ Ritt nicht mehr zurück. 16. _____ Fischer
brachte _____ Fang zum Hotel. 17. Er verlor _____ Halt auf dem Eis
_____ Gletschers, und dann kam _____ Sturz in _____ Tiefe.
18. _____ Stich _____ Biene ist schmerzhaft. 19. _das_ Kindermäd-
chen, _der_ Chauffeur, _der_ Koch, _der_ Gärtner und _die_ Sekretärin gratulierten Herrn Meier. 20. _der_ Leopard trug _die_ Antilope
auf einen Baum. 21. _die_ Geschichte _der_ Sklaverei beginnt im
Altertum. 22. _die_ Infektion macht dich so müde. 23. _der_
Buddhismus ist _die_ Weltreligion. 24. Was für _einen_ Motor ist das?
25. Heute sagt man in Deutschland: _der_ Teenager. Früher sagte man
die Jugendliche. 26. _die_ Schwimmen in _dem_ Fluß ist verboten.
27. _die_ Oder-Neiße-Linie ist heute _eine_ Ostgrenze Deutschlands.
28. _der_ Rhein und _die_ Donau sind Deutschlands größte Flüsse.
29. _das_ alte Hamburg liegt an _der_ Elbe. 30. _das_ alte Europa
existiert kaum noch.

E.19 *Give the definite article:*

1. _der_ Herr. 2. _die_ alte Spanien. 3. _die_ Donau. 4. _die_
Kusine. 5. _der_ Tornado. 6. _der_ Schweiz. 7. _die_ Dumm-
heit. 8. _der_ Pragmatismus. 9. _die_ Tänzerin. 10. _der_ Lieb-
ling. 11. _der_ Gladiator. 12. _der_ Bäcker. 13. _die_ Zuschau-
erin. 14. _die_ Krankheit. 15. _der_ Neckar. 16. _der_ Hagel.
17. _das_ New York. 18. _das_ moderne London. 19. _das_ Weiß
des Kleides. 20. _der_ deutsche 1. 21. _die_ Blau ihrer Augen.
22. _das_ Ladenschild. 23. _das_ Stadium. 24. _das_ Fensterchen.
25. _der_ König. 26. _das_ H$_2$O. 27. _der_ Vetter. 28. _____

Vier. 29. _____ Red Owl (*cigar*). 30. _____ geteilte Berlin.
31. _____ englische th. 32. _____ Natrium. 33. _____ Havanna.
34. _____ Rhein. 35. _____ Geologie. 36. _____ Konditorei.
37. _____ Privateingang. 38. _____ Neue. 39. _____ Schwimmer.
40. _____ Rechnung. 41. _____ Induktor. 42. Nur _____ Hier und
Jetzt kümmert mich. 43. _____ Operation. 44. _____ Tapferkeit.
45. _____ Rheumatismus. 46. _____ A. 47. _____ Arche Noahs.
48. _____ Eisen. 49. _____ Schrei. 50. _____ Spieler. 51. _____
Winter. 52. _____ Stierkämpfer. 53. _____ Kreta Homers.
54. _____ Abend. 55. _____ Theologe. 56. _____ Dezember.
57. _____ Zuschauer. 58. _____ Vater. 59. _____ Reaktionär.
60. _____ Dienstag. 61. _____ Süden. 62. _____ Demokrat.
63. _____ Smaragd. 64. _____ Führer. 65. _____ Neffe. 66. _____
Berlin. 67. _____ Weinen. 68. _____ Operation. 69. _____ Fünf.
70. _____ C. 71. _____ Athlet. 72. _____ Schwimmerin. 73. _____
Konfirmation. 74. _____ Regierung. 75. _____ Regierungsgebäude.
76. _____ Kirche. 77. _____ Biene. 78. _____ Gesundheit.
79. _____ Tanz. 80. _____ Puppe. 81. _____ Trinken. 82. _____
Blitz. 83. _____ Donner. 84. _____ Wolke. 85. _____ Ladenfräu-
lein. 86. _____ Leukämie. 87. _____ Organismus. 88. _____ Studium. 89. _____ Fleischerei. 90. _____ Frauchen. 91. _____ Nordsee. 92. _____ Michigan See. 93. _____ Legion. 94. _____ Le-
gionär.

20. Plural of Nouns

a. Monosyllabics

SINGULAR	der Baum	der Bleistift	die Stadt	das Tor
PLURAL	die Bäume	die Bleistifte	die Städte	die Tore

Most nouns of one syllable add **-e** in the plural, whether used by them-
selves or as the last part of a compound noun (**Bleistift**). Feminines also
add umlaut, neuters do not. Almost all masculine nouns in common use
add umlaut. The few exceptions worth remembering are:

der Arm, der Hund, der Punkt, der Schuh, der Tag

b. Polysyllabics

	(1)	(2)	(3)	(4)
SINGULAR	der Garten	der Deutsche	der Student	die Frage
PLURAL	die Gärten	die Deutschen	die Studenten	die Fragen

Most nouns of more than one syllable (polysyllabics) form the plural as follows:

1. Masculines and neuters ending in **-er, -en, -el** and neuters in **-chen, -lein** add no ending. Some masculines umlaut the stem vowel, neuters do not. Examples:

   der Garten, die Gärten; das Ufer, die Ufer

2. Masculines and neuters ending in **-e** add **-n.** Examples:

   der Deutsche, die Deutschen; das Auge, die Augen

3. Masculines of non-German origin with accent on the last syllable and nouns ending in **-or** add **-en.** Examples:

   der Student, die Studenten; der Professor, die Professoren

4. All feminines of more than one syllable add **-(e)n.** Nouns ending in **-in** add **-nen.** Examples:

   die Frage, die Fragen; die Schwester, die Schwestern; die Antwort, die Antworten; die Stellung, die Stellungen; die Amerikanerin, die Amerikanerinnen

Observe:

Polysyllabic masculine and neuter nouns not belonging to the above categories add **-e,** unless their last component is one of the exceptional nouns listed below.

c. "Irregular" Monosyllabics

1. Monosyllabic masculines, feminines, and neuters forming the plural in **-en:**

der Christ, die Christen	*Christian*
der Fürst, die Fürsten	*prince*
der Graf, die Grafen	*count*
der Held, die Helden	*hero*
der Herr, die Herren	*gentleman*
der Mensch, die Menschen	*man, people*
die Art, die Arten	*kind*
die Fahrt, die Fahrten	*ride*
die Frau, die Frauen	*woman*
die Pflicht, die Pflichten	*duty*
die Schlacht, die Schlachten	*battle*
die Schuld, die Schulden	*debt*
die Tat, die Taten	*deed*
die Tür, die Türen	*door*

die Uhr, die Uhren	*watch*
die Welt, die Welten	*world*
die Zahl, die Zahlen	*figure*
die Zeit, die Zeiten	*time*

2. Monosyllabic masculines and neuters forming their plural in **-er,** adding umlaut where possible:

der Mann, die Männer	*man*
der Wald, die Wälder	*forest*
das Bad, die Bäder	*bath*
das Bild, die Bilder	*picture*
das Blatt, die Blätter	*leaf*
das Buch, die Bücher	*book*
das Dorf, die Dörfer	*village*
das Ei, die Eier	*egg*
das Fach, die Fächer	*(school) subject*
das Feld, die Felder	*field*
das Glas, die Gläser	*glass*
das Haus, die Häuser	*house*
das Huhn, die Hühner	*chicken*
das Kind, die Kinder	*child*
das Kleid, die Kleider	*dress*
das Land, die Länder	*country*
das Licht, die Lichter	*light*
das Lied, die Lieder	*song*
das Schloß, die Schlösser	*castle*
das Tal, die Täler	*valley*
das Volk, die Völker	*people*
das Wort, die Wörter	*word*

d. "Irregular" Polysyllabics

der Nachbar, die Nachbarn	*neighbor*
die Mutter, die Mütter	*mother*
die Tochter, die Töchter	*daughter*
das Gebäude, die Gebäude	*building*
das Gebirge, die Gebirge	*mountain range*

Exercise

E.20 *Form the plural of the following nouns:*

1. der Turm. 2. die Kraft. 3. das Ziel. 4. der Damenschuh. 5. die

Kleinstadt. 6. das Theaterstück. 7. der Entschluß. 8. das Bein.
9. der Tag. 10. der Mann. 11. das Land. 12. der Fremdling. 13. der
Deckel. 14. der Hafen. 15. der Berliner. 16. der Brunnen. 17. der
Frankfurter. 18. die Tochter. 19. das Kätzchen. 20. die Bewegung.
21. die Schwimmerin. 22. die Mutter. 23. die Fahrt. 24. der Chinese.
25. der Konfirmand. 26. die Legion. 27. der Bäcker. 28. der Faktor.
29. das Schloß. 30. die Mutter. 31. das Sternchen. 32. das Licht.
33. die Schlacht. 34. die Kraft. 35. der Stoß. 36. die Vorlesung.
37. der Christ. 38. der Löwe. 39. die Löwin. 40. der Boxer. 41. das
Glas. 42. das Boot. 43. der Haifisch. 44. der Einbruch. 45. der Einbrecher. 46. das Volksfest. 47. die Morgenzeitung. 48. das Gespräch.
49. die Adresse. 50. der Berg. 51. die Kunst. 52. die Übung. 53. die
Reise. 54. die Torheit. 55. die Französin. 56. das Veilchen. 57. das
Tier. 58. der Künstler. 59. der Säugling. 60. das Gebirge. 61. der
Fähnrich. 62. die Bäckerei. 63. die Philosophie. 64. der Wald.
65. das Dorf. 66. das Haus. 67. das Schwarzbrot. 68. der Durchbruch. 69. das Lied. 70. das Gebäude.

21. Declension of Nouns

a. Masculines and Neuters

PLURAL ENDING: (⸚)e		PLURAL: NO ENDING	
der Baum	das Tier	der Garten	das Fenster
des Baumes	des Tieres	des Gartens	des Fensters
dem Baum(e)	dem Tier(e)	dem Garten	dem Fenster
den Baum	das Tier	den Garten	das Fenster
die Bäume	die Tiere	die Gärten	die Fenster
der Bäume	der Tiere	der Gärten	der Fenster
den Bäumen	den Tieren	den Gärten	den Fenstern
die Bäume	die Tiere	die Gärten	die Fenster

PLURAL ENDING: ⸚er	
der Mann	das Land
des Mannes	des Landes
dem Mann(e)	dem Land(e)
den Mann	das Land
die Männer	die Länder
der Männer	der Länder
den Männern	den Ländern
die Männer	die Länder

Observe:

1. In the genitive singular, masculine and neuter nouns add **s** (nouns of one syllable normally add **-es**).

2. In the dative plural, nouns add **-n,** unless the nominative plural already ends in **-n (Gärten).**

3. In the dative singular, monosyllabic masculine and neuter nouns sometimes end in **-e: im Haus** or **im Hause.** This ending is not mandatory.

b. Feminines

PLURAL ENDING: **-e**	PLURAL ENDING: **-(e)n**
die Stadt	die Frage
der Stadt	der Frage
der Stadt	der Frage
die Stadt	die Frage
die Städte	die Fragen
der Städte	der Fragen
den Städten	den Fragen
die Städte	die Fragen

Observe:

Feminines do not add endings in the singular. Feminines whose plural ends in **-e** add **-n** in the dative plural.

c. Special Group A

der Mensch	der Junge
des Menschen	des Jungen
dem Menschen	dem Jungen
den Menschen	den Jungen
die Menschen	die Jungen
der Menschen	der Jungen
den Menschen	den Jungen
die Menschen	die Jungen

The above examples illustrate the declensional pattern of a fairly large group of masculine nouns whose plurals end in **-en.** Such nouns have **-en** or **-n** in every case except the nominative singular.

Observe:

der Herr, des Herrn, dem Herrn, den Herrn; but the plural is **die Herren,**

etc. The word **Herr** ends in **-n** in all singular forms except the nominative.

d. Special Group B

The following common nouns add **-(e)s** in the genitive singular and **-(e)n** in the plural:

NOM.	GEN.	PLURAL
der Bauer	des Bauers[1]	die Bauern
der Nachbar	des Nachbars[2]	die Nachbarn
der Schmerz	des Schmerzes	die Schmerzen
der Staat	des Staates	die Staaten
das Auge	des Auges	die Augen
das Bett	des Bettes	die Betten
das Hemd	des Hemdes	die Hemden
das Ohr	des Ohres	die Ohren

To this group also belong all masculine nouns ending in **-or**:

der Doktor	des Doktors	die Doktoren
der Professor	des Professors	die Professoren
der Motor	des Motors	die Motoren

e. Special Group C

The following nouns are irregular in the singular:

der Gedanke, des Gedankens, dem Gedanken, den Gedanken; Plural: **die Gedanken,** etc.;

der Name, des Namens, dem Namen, den Namen; Plural: **die Namen,** etc.;

das Herz, des Herzens, dem Herz(en), das Herz; Plural: **die Herzen,** etc.;

das Bett, des Bettes, dem Bett, das Bett; Plural: **die Betten,** etc.

f. Special Group D

Many words of non-German origin (mostly English and French words) retain their original plural **-s.** In the singular, such words add **-s** in the genitive; in the plural, all forms end in **-s.** Examples:

das Auto, die Autos; das Café, die Cafés; das Hotel, die Hotels; das Restaurant, die Restaurants; das Reisebüro, die Reisebüros

---

[1] Modern German prefers: des Bauern.
[2] Modern German prefers: des Nachbarn.

Exercises

E.21 *Form genitive relations between the following nouns:*

EXAMPLE: das Haus, der Nachbar
            das Haus des Nachbars

1. das Leben, der Soldat. 2. die Bedeutung, der Traum. 3. das Spezialgebiet, der Professor. 4. der Kapitän, das Schiff. 5. der Geschmack,
die Frucht. 6. die Frau, der Russe. 7. die Anatomie, das Fischauge.
8. der Name, der Student. 9. die Entdeckung, der Physiker. 10. der
Ruhm, der Zoologe. 11. der Wert, die Freiheit. 12. der Glaube, der
Christ. 13. das Leben, der Held. 14. die Armut, die Frau. 15. der
Besitzer, das Feld. 16. der Name, der Bauer. 17. der Preis, der Wagen.
18. der Glanz, das Licht. 19. die Schnelligkeit, das Motorrad. 20. die
Schönheit, die Sommernacht. 21. die Lage, der Eingang.

E.22 *Supply the dative plural of the following nouns:*

1. in den (Garten). 2. mit den (Rose). 3. Geben Sie es den (Kind).
4. in diesen (Land). 5. aus diesen (Dorf). 6. in diesen (Tag). 7. in
diesen (Dorf). 8. unter den (Baum). 9. aus seinen (Brief). 10. Glauben
Sie solchen (Prophet)? 11. von unseren modernen (Komponist). 12. mit
solchen (Mensch). 13. von den (Großmacht). 14. mit vielen (Licht).
15. bei den (Schweizer). 16. mit unseren (Arbeiter). 17. Sagen Sie das
unseren (Studentin)! 18. mit ihren (Tochter). 19. in vielen (Stadt).
20. auf den (Berg). 21. mit vier (Motor).

22. Prepositions

a. Prepositions with the Genitive

(an)statt	*instead of*	**anstatt des Wassers**
außerhalb	*outside*	**außerhalb der Stadt**
diesseits	*on this side of*	**diesseits des Flusses**
infolge	*as a result of*	**infolge des Krieges**
innerhalb	*inside, within*	**innerhalb der Stadt; innerhalb einer Woche**
jenseits	*on the other side of*	**jenseits des Flusses**
oberhalb	*above, higher up*	**oberhalb des Dorfes; oberhalb des Flusses**
trotz	*in spite of*	**trotz des schlechten Wetters**
unterhalb	*below*	**unterhalb der Brücke**
während	*during*	**während der Nacht**
wegen	*because of*	**wegen der Kälte**

b. Prepositions with the Dative

aus	*out of*	Er kommt **aus dem Haus.**
	from	Er kommt **aus dem Süden.**
	of	Es ist **aus grünem Glas.**
bei	*at (the home of)*	Er wohnt **bei seinem Onkel.**
	near	Das Hotel ist nah **beim Bahnhof.**
mit	*with*	Sie ging **mit ihm.**
nach	*to(ward)*	Wir fahren **nach Deutschland.**
	after	Wer kam **nach Ihnen?**
seit	*since*	**seit dem Krieg**
	for	**Seit einer Woche** ist er hier.
von	*from*	Das Flugzeug kommt **von Berlin.**
	by	Ein Lied **von Schubert.**
		Es wurde **von ihm** komponiert.
zu	*to*	Ich gehe **zum Arzt** / **zum Bahnhof** / **zur Post** / **zu Bett.**

c. Prepositions with the Accusative

bis	*until*	Ich bleibe **bis nächsten Sonntag.**
	to	von Montag **bis Donnerstag**
	as far as	Wir sind **bis Bonn** gefahren.
	by	**Bis Sonntag** bin ich wieder zurück.
durch	*through*	Er ging **durch das Zimmer.**
	by	Er wurde **durch eine Bombe** getötet.
für	*for*	Das ist genug **für heute.**
	for the benefit of	Er hat sehr viel **für mich** getan.
gegen	*against*	Er hat es **gegen meinen Wunsch** getan.
	toward	**gegen fünf Uhr**
ohne	*without*	Gehen Sie nicht **ohne mich!**
um	*around*	Er ging **um das Haus** herum.
	at	**um fünf Uhr**
	about	**um 1940**
wider	*against*	Er hat es **wider meinen Willen** getan.

d. Prepositions with the Dative or Accusative

an	*on* (vertically)
	at, to, by
auf	*on* (horizontally)
hinter	*behind*
in	*in, into*
neben	*near, next to, beside*
über	*over*
unter	*under, among*

vor   *in front of, before*
zwischen   *between*

Das Bild hängt **an der Wand.** Er hängt das Bild **an die Wand.**
Er saß **auf dem Stuhl.** Er setzte sich **auf den Stuhl.**
Er ging **im Zimmer** auf und ab. Er ging **ins Zimmer.**

The above prepositions are used with the dative to indicate location or
movement at a place, and with the accusative to indicate movement to
a place.

Observe:

If the definite article is not serving as a demonstrative, the preposition
forms a contraction with it whenever possible:

Er ist **im** Hotel. Er ging **ins** Hotel.
Er saß **am** Klavier. Er ging **ans** Klavier. Legen Sie es **aufs** Klavier.
Der Stein flog **durchs** Fenster; er kam **vom** Parkplatz.
Wir gehen **zum** Fußballspiel.
Diese Straße führt **zur** Oper.

e. Idiomatic expressions involving prepositions with the dative or accusative:

Observe:

If the meaning of the verb does not permit distinction between location
and movement, the dative is used after **an, in, unter, vor, zwischen;** the
accusative after **auf** and **über.**

1. **an** and dative

   am Morgen / Abend   *in the morning / evening*
   an Ihrer Stelle   *in your place*
   ein Professor **an der Universität**   *a professor at the university*
   Er hat keinen Mangel **an Geld.**   *He has no lack of money.*

2. **an** and accusative

   Wir reisen **ans Meer.**   *We are going to the seashore.*
   Wir kommen bald **an den Rhein.**   *We'll soon come to the Rhine.*

3. **auf** and dative

   Ich war **auf der Post / Bank.**   *I was at the post office / bank.*
   Er wohnt **auf dem Land.**   *He lives in the country.*

4. **auf** and accusative

Ich gehe **auf die Post / Bank / Universität.**	*I am going to the post office / bank / university.*
Er ist **aufs Land** gezogen.	*He moved to the country.*
auf diese Weise	*in this way*
auf jeden Fall	*in any case*
Sag's **auf deutsch!**	*Say it in German.*
eine Antwort **auf die Frage / den Brief**	*an answer to the question / the letter*
auf den ersten Blick	*at first sight*

5. **in** and dative

Ich wohne **in der Nähe.**	*I live nearby.*
im Augenblick	*at this moment*
im Durchschnitt	*on the average*
Sie lebt **im Ausland.**	*She lives abroad.*
im Radio / Fernsehen	*on the radio / television*
im allgemeinen	*in general, as a rule*

6. **in** and accusative

Sie fuhr **in die Schweiz.**	*She went to Switzerland.*
Er ging **ins Theater / Kino / Konzert / Büro.**	*He went to the theater / movies / concert / office.*
bis spät **in die Nacht**	*till late at night*
Er hat sich **in den Finger** geschnitten.	*He cut his finger.*

7. **über** and accusative

Er fuhr **über Köln** nach Bonn.	*He went to Bonn via Cologne.*
tagsüber	*in the daytime*
heute **übers Jahr**	*a year (from) today*
ein Scheck **über 100 Dollar**	*a check for 100 dollars*

8. **unter** and dative

unter den Leuten	*among the people*
unter anderem	*among other things*
unter uns (gesagt)	*between ourselves*
unter dieser Bedingung	*on this condition*

9. **vor** and dative

vor vielen Jahren	*many years ago*
heute **vor acht Tagen**	*a week ago today*
vor allem	*above all*
Sie weinte **vor Freude.**	*She cried for joy.*
Er zitterte **vor Furcht.**	*He was trembling with fear.*

Exercises

E.23 *Genitive:*

1. wegen (sein schwaches Herz). 2. während (unsere schönen Sommerferien). 3. trotz (seine kräftige Konstitution). 4. innerhalb (der häusliche Kreis). 5. oberhalb (der kleine Bach). 6. statt (ein hübsches Geschenk). 7. diesseits (die polnische Grenze). 8. unterhalb (das kleine Dorf). 9. wegen (der starke Sturm). 10. während (die ganze Nacht). 11. trotz (seine vielen Verluste). 12. trotz (mein gutgemeinter Rat). 13. wegen (ihre alte Mutter).

E.24 *Dative—Use contractions wherever possible:*

1. aus (seine kleine Wohnung). 2. von (der alte Kontinent). 3. mit (ihr berühmter Mann). 4. nach (vier lange Jahre). 5. bei (seine nächsten Verwandten). 6. seit (ein halber Monat). 7. von (einige gute Freunde). 8. von (der höchste Berg). 9. zu (sein kleiner Sohn). 10. zu (das erste Mal). 11. in (dieses alte Haus). 12. in (das kleine Zimmer). 13. an (der nächste Tisch). 14. in (sein neues Auto). 15. in (die europäischen Zeitungen). 16. auf (die andere Seite). 17. an (der nächste Sonntag). 18. an (der wolkenlose Himmel). 19. in (das tiefe Meer). 20. in (der blaue See).

E.25 *Accusative—Use contractions wherever possible:*

1. durch (eine kleine Straße). 2. für (ein amerikanischer Student). 3. durch (das nächste Dorf). 4. gegen (dein böser Husten). 5. ohne (ein roter Pfennig). 6. für (das liebe tägliche Brot). 7. um (die kleine Stadt). 8. in (das kalte Wasser). 9. um (das liebe Leben). 10. ohne (ein deutscher Paß). 11. für (ein Kranker). 12. ohne (die moderne Medizin). 13. für (eine Kranke). 14. durch (das ganze Leben). 15. gegen (die schnelle Strömung). 16. wider (das ewige Gesetz). 17. ohne (seine deutschen Verwandten). 18. in (der alte Park). 19. in (das wilde Meer). 20. wider (sein eigener Wille).

E.26 *Dative or accusative—Use the preposition **in** before the words in parentheses. Use contractions wherever possible:*

1. Ist er noch (dasselbe Hotel)? 2. Das Dorf liegt (ein schönes Tal). 3. Das Flugzeug stürzte (das Meer). 4. Wir fuhren mit dem Auto (die nächste Stadt). 5. Was stand (sein letzter Brief)? 6. Wir fanden ihn (seine neue Wohnung). 7. Wölfe erscheinen oft (der westliche Teil Polens). 8. Jeden Sommer fuhr meine Familie (die deutschen Alpen).

9. Wir schwammen eine halbe Stunde (das kühle, klare Wasser). 10. Wir badeten jeden Morgen (das blaue Mittelmeer). 11. Er stieg (der nächste Zug). 12. Der Baum war (der Fluß) gestürzt.

E.27 *Use* **auf** *before the parentheses and contractions wherever possible:*

1. Der Baum liegt (die Garage). 2. Der Baum stürzte (die Garage). 3. Die Soldaten schossen (der Zug). 4. Er stellte das Glas (der Tisch). 5. Er schlug mit der Faust (der Tisch). 6. Die Sonne warf einen breiten roten Streifen (das Wasser). 7. Die Boote tanzten (das wilde Wasser). 8. Der Berliner Zug steht (derselbe Bahnsteig). 9. Legen Sie Ihre Sachen bitte (das Bett)! 10. Er liegt noch (das Bett) und schläft. 11. Er legte sich den Sack (die breite Schulter). 12. Er trug den Verwundeten (seine breiten Schultern). 13. In Süddeutschland haben viele Bauern Storchnester (die Dächer ihrer Häuser). 14. Schreiben Sie die Adresse bitte (dieser Zettel)!

E.28 *Use* **an** *before the parentheses and contractions wherever possible:*

1. Die Deutschen hängen nicht nur Glaskugeln, sondern auch Süßigkeiten (der Weihnachtsbaum). 2. Sie banden den Gefangenen (ein Baum). 3. Fahr das Boot (das Ufer)! 4. Die Boote sind alle (das Ufer). 5. Er klopfte laut (die Tür). 6. Ein Zettel hing (die Tür). 7. Die kleinen Jungen hielten sich (die Straßenbahn) fest. 8. Er hielt den Stier (der Nasenring) fest. 9. Hält der Bremer Zug (diese Station)? 10. Das Schwert des Damokles hing (ein Pferdehaar). 11. Dort steht er (das Fenster). 12. Bitte lehnen Sie sich nicht (diese Wand)! 13. Im Sommer fahren wir (das Meer). 14. Wir fahren jetzt (der Rhein). 15. Jetzt komme ich (die Reihe).

E.29 *Use* **über** *before the parentheses and contractions wherever possible:*

1. Das Flugzeug flog hoch (die Wolken) im herrlichen Blau. 2. Die Rakete stieg (die Atmosphäre) hinaus. 3. Der fliehende Ostberliner stieg (die Mauer). 4. Er schwamm (die Donau). 5. Das Buch heißt „Im Segelboot (der Atlantische Ozean)". 6. Wir haben es gesehen; die fliegende Untertasse schwebte zehn Minuten (unser Städtchen). 7. Gießen Sie die Butter langsam (das Huhn)! 8. Schweißtropfen liefen ihm (das Gesicht). 9. Die Tränen liefen ihm (die Wangen). 10. Er stolperte (die Schreibmaschine) auf dem Boden. 11. Die Leute (unser Schlafzimmer) machen zu viel Lärm.

E.30 *Use* **unter** *before the parentheses and contractions wherever possible:*

1. Die Garage ist (das Haus). 2. Wo ist die Katze? Sie ist wahrscheinlich (das Sofa) gekrochen. 3. Dieser Fluß fließt (die Erde) weiter. 4. Ich habe mir ein Stückchen Holz (der Nagel) gerammt. 5. Ich kann nicht (dasselbe Dach) mit ihm wohnen. 6. Wir standen (die Bäume), bis der Regen aufhörte. 7. Ich freue mich darauf, daß wir bald wieder festen Boden (die Füße) haben werden. 8. Stecken Sie sich das Fieberthermometer (die Zunge)! 9. Ich habe eine schmerzhafte Stelle (die Zunge). 10. Bald werden wir (die Sterne) eines südlichen Himmels sehen. 11. Sie haben die Bilder in einem Bunker tief (die Erde) gefunden. 12. Er legte den Brief schnell (sein Buch). 13. Kommen Sie hierher (der Baum)! 14. Sie warfen Handgranaten (die Brücke).

E.31 *Use* **hinter** *or* **neben** *before the parentheses and contractions wherever possible:*

1. Die Garage ist (das alte Haus). 2. Das Bild ist (das Sofa) gefallen. 3. Die Bomben fielen (der amerikanische Flugzeugträger). 4. Die Motorboote fuhren (der amerikanische Passagierdampfer) in den Hafen. 5. Fritz setzte sich (die mysteriöse Dame). 6. Die Kavallerie wartete (die vorderste Linie). 7. Fahren Sie das Auto (die Garage)! 8. Parken Sie Ihr Auto (das blaue Auto) da! 9. Ich saß die ganze Zeit (ein dicker, großer Herr). 10. (die Dame) im Pelzmantel ist noch Platz.

23. Personal Pronouns

SINGULAR

NOM.	ich	du	Sie	er	sie	es
GEN.	meiner	deiner	Ihrer	seiner	ihrer	seiner
DAT.	mir	dir	Ihnen	ihm	ihr	ihm
ACC.	mich	dich	Sie	ihn	sie	es

PLURAL

NOM.	wir	ihr	Sie	sie
GEN.	unser	euer	Ihrer	ihrer
DAT.	uns	euch	Ihnen	ihnen
ACC.	uns	euch	Sie	sie

a. When a pronoun is used with a preposition and refers to one or more objects, the pronoun is replaced by **da-** (**dar-** before a vowel) and combined with the preposition: **damit** (*with it / them*), **darauf** (*on it / them*).

Example:

Er hat einen scharfen Schmerz / scharfe Schmerzen im Ellbogen.
He has a sharp pain / sharp pains in his elbow.
Er sollte etwas **dagegen** tun.
He should do something for it / them.

b. In addition to their literal meanings some of these **da**-compounds have acquired special meanings:

dabei	*in so doing, at the same time*
dagegen	*on the other hand*
damit	*in order that* (as dependent conjunction)
darum	*therefore*
dazu	*in addition*

24. Reflexive Pronouns

ich frage mich	**Ich kaufe mir** eine Zeitung.
I ask myself	*I buy myself a newspaper.*
du fragst dich	**Du kaufst dir** eine Zeitung.
you ask yourself	*You buy yourself a newspaper.*
er fragt sich	**Er kauft sich** eine Zeitung.
he asks himself	*He buys himself a newspaper.*
sie fragt sich	**Sie kauft sich** eine Zeitung.
she asks herself	*She buys herself a newspaper.*
wir fragen uns	**Wir kaufen uns** eine Zeitung.
we ask ourselves	*We buy ourselves a newspaper.*
ihr fragt euch	**Ihr kauft euch** eine Zeitung.
you ask yourselves	*You buy yourselves a newspaper.*
sie fragen sich	**Sie kaufen sich** eine Zeitung.
they ask themselves	*They buy themselves a newspaper.*
Sie fragen sich	**Sie kaufen sich** eine Zeitung.
you ask yourself (yourselves)	*You buy yourself (yourselves) a newspaper.*

a. The dative reflexive pronoun is also used to indicate the possessor of parts of the body or clothing:

Ich wasche **mir** die Hände.	*I wash my hands.*
Sie zog **sich** ein Kleid an.	*She put on her dress.*

b. **Selbst** is often used to strengthen the reflexive pronoun:

Der Kleine hat **sich selbst** angezogen.
The little one dressed by himself.

Exercises

E.32 *Supply* **mir** *or* **mich:**

1. Ich frage _____ oft, warum. 2. Ich habe _dich_ hingesetzt. 3. Ich kann _____ das nicht vorstellen. 4. Ich muß _____ waschen. 5. Ich ärgere _mir_ über ihn. 6. Das kann ich _____ denken.

E.33 *Change the sentences in E.32 to questions, supplying* **dir** *or* **dich:**

E.34 *Change the sentences in accordance with the subjects indicated:*

1. Sie bestellt sich eine Tasse Tee. (ich, wir, er). 2. Er freut sich, daß wir kommen. (Frau Schmidt, die Kinder). 3. Setzen Sie sich! (Fritz, Hans und Paul). 4. Ich werde mich gut anziehen. (wir, Ilse, meine Freundinnen). 5. Herr Heinz möchte sich einen Gebrauchtwagen kaufen. (meine Eltern, ich). 6. Bereitet er sich auf den Arztberuf vor? (du, Sie, Ihr Freund).

E.35 *Write in German:*

1. She bought herself a new dress. 2. He is interested in her, but she is not interested in him. 3. Is he having a good time in the city? 4. He was glad that they had hurried. 5. Don't worry about it! (Fritz, Hans and Paul, Mr. Schmidt). 6. Has he shaved already? 7. I know that she is mistaken. 8. He lay down. 9. He is preparing himself for a trip to Europe. 10. I want to take a look at the cathedral.

Vocabulary:

1. sich bedienen. 2. sich interessieren für. 3. sich amüsieren. 4. sich beeilen. 5. sich sorgen. 6. sich rasieren. 7. sich irren. 8. sich hinlegen. 9. sich vorbereiten auf. 10. sich ansehen.

25. Relative Pronouns

| | SINGULAR | | | PLURAL | |
	M.	F.	N.	M.F.N.	
NOM.	der	die	das	die	who; which, that
GEN.	dessen	deren	dessen	deren	whose; of which
DAT.	dem	der	dem	denen	to whom; to which
ACC.	den	die	das	die	whom; which, that

NOM.	welcher	welche	welches	welche
GEN.	(dessen)	(deren)	(dessen)	(deren)
DAT.	welchem	welcher	welchem	welchen
ACC.	welchen	welche	welches	welche

a. Of the two relative pronouns **der** and **welcher,** only **der** is used in spoken German.

b. The relative pronoun agrees in gender and number with the noun to which it refers; its case is determined by its function in the clause:

Das ist also **der Schwarzwald, von dem** ich so viel gehört habe.
This then is the Black Forest of which I have heard so much.
Die Hügel da hinten, **die** die Karte nicht zeigt, sind die Ausläufer der Alpen.
The hills back there, which the map doesn't show, are the foothills of the Alps.

c. The relative pronoun may never be omitted in German:

Die Hügel, die du da hinten siehst, sind die Ausläufer der Alpen.
The hills you see back there are the foothills of the Alps.

Observe: A relative clause is always set off by commas.

Exercises

E.36 *Supply the correct relative pronoun:*

1. Der Turm, _der_ früher dort gestanden hatte, war nicht mehr da.
2. Man hat uns ein Hotel empfohlen, _dessen_ Besitzer Deutschschweizer ist. 3. Die Schweiz, _deren_ Bevölkerung aus Deutschen, Franzosen und Italienern besteht, hat das Problem der Koexistenz schon lange gelöst.
4. Entschuldigen Sie bitte, aber die Feder mit _der_ Sie schreiben, gehört mir. 5. Die Kleider, _die_ ich mir gerne kaufen möchte, sind immer zu teuer. 6. Das Haus, in _dem_ wir wohnen, ist etwa 50 Jahre alt. 7. Die Nachrichten, _die_ uns Presse, Radio und Fernsehen senden, sind meist trauriger Art. 8. Vögel, _die_ am Morgen singen, holt am Abend die Katze. 9. Das war eine Sekretärin meines Vaters, an _die_ ich mich nicht erinnere. 10. Das sind Dinge, an _die_ ich mich nicht mehr erinnere.

E.37 *Combine the sentences to make the second a relative clause:*

EXAMPLE:

Der Kodiakbär ist Amerikas größtes Landtier. Man findet den Kodiak-
bären nur in Alaska.
Der Kodiakbär, den man nur in Alaska findet, ist Amerikas größtes
Landtier.

1. Endlich besuchten wir auch den Schwarzwald. Jeder Reiseführer lobt
den Schwarzwald. 2. Baron von Steuben ist in Deutschland unbekannt.
Jedes amerikanische Schulkind kennt von Steuben. 3. Ich habe Sehnsucht nach dem Bayrischen Wald. Ich habe als Kind Blaubeeren im
Bayrischen Wald gepflückt. 4. Nietzsche ist ein deutscher Philosoph.
Die meisten Nichtdeutschen haßten in früheren Jahren Nietzsche, den
Philosophen. 5. Das sind Leute. Ich kann mit den Leuten nicht arbeiten.
6. Hier ist ein Chemiker. Seine Experimente sind sehr berühmt. 7. Auch
in Deutschland gibt es viele Studenten. Das Studium der Studenten wird
vom Staat bezahlt. 8. Das alte Nürnberg ist im Weltkrieg zerstört
worden. Seine Mauern stehen zum Teil noch. 9. Er ist einer von den
charmanten Männern. Keiner traut den Männern. 10. Ich gebe dir die
Adresse meiner Sekretärin. Ohne die Hilfe der Sekretärin könnte ich
nicht mehr auskommen.

26. Interrogative Pronouns

a. Direct Interrogative Pronouns

	MASCULINE AND FEMININE		NEUTER	
NOM.	**wer**	*who*	**was**	*what*
GEN.	**wessen**	*of whom*	**wessen**	*of what*
DAT.	**wem**	*(to) whom*	—	
ACC.	**wen**	*whom*	**was**	*what*

Wer ist der Herr in dem blauen Anzug?
Who is the gentleman in the blue suit?
Was will er?
What does he want?

b. Indirect Interrogative Pronouns

Wissen Sie, **wer** der Herr im blauen Anzug ist?
Do you know who the gentleman in the blue suit is?

Sagen Sie mir, **was** er will!
Tell me what he wants.

c. Interrogative Pronoun **was** with Prepositions

With prepositions, the interrogative pronoun **was** becomes **wo(r):**

Womit hat er dich geschlagen?
With what did he strike you?
Woran denkst du die ganze Zeit?
What are you thinking of all the time?

27. Interrogative Adjectives

welcher *which* (declined like **der**-word)

was für ein *what kind of* (declined like **ein**-word)

Welchen Film haben Sie gesehen?
Which film did you see?
In **was für einem Hotel** haben Sie gewohnt?
In what kind of hotel did you stay?
In **was für Hotels** haben Sie gewohnt?
In what kind of hotels did you stay?

28. Wer and Was as Indefinite Relative Pronouns

a. Without Antecedent

Wer sie kennt, mag sie.
He who (whoever) knows her, likes her.
Was er gesagt hat, ist wahr.
What (that which) he said is true.

b. Was after Indefinite Pronouns: **alles, etwas, nichts, vieles**

Hast du **alles, was** du brauchst?
Do you have everything (that) you need?
Ich sehe hier **nichts, was** mich interessiert.
I see nothing here that interests me.

c. Was is used to refer to an entire clause:

Sie wird leicht müde, was mir Sorgen macht.
She tires easily, (a fact) which worries me.

d. Was is used after an indefinite superlative:

Das ist **das Beste, was** ich für Sie tun kann.
This is the best (that) I can do for you.

e. When **was,** referring to an indefinite antecedent, is governed by a preposition, **wo(r)** plus preposition must be used:

Ist das alles, **woran** du denken kannst?
Is that all of which you can think? or Is that all you can think of?

Exercise

E.38 *Supply the correct forms of* **welcher, was für ein, was, wer:**

1. Es ist nicht alles Gold, _was_ glänzt. 2. In _welchem_ Kino wird dieser Film gezeigt? 3. Glaubst du alles, _____ in der Zeitung steht? 4. _____ erwartest du, Peter? 5. Mein Junge ißt sehr wenig, _was_ mir Sorgen macht. 6. Für _welchen_ Film interessieren Sie sich? 7. Das Schönste, _was_ ich in Rom gesehen habe, war das römische Forum im Mondlicht. 8. Was _für_ Leute sind das? 9. _____ hat das gesagt? Shakespeare? 10. Das ist etwas, _was_ ich nicht verstehe. 11. _vor_ über spricht er morgen in der Vorlesung? 12. Auf _____ wartest du? Auf Heidi? 13. Ich glaube nicht ein Wort von allem, _____ er uns da erzählt hat. 14. Weißt du nicht, _____ für wir kämpfen? 15. Was _____ Film ist „Der Untergang des Römischen Reiches"? 16. _____ das gesagt hat, kennt das Leben. 17. Er klagt oft über seine Frau, _____ ich nicht verstehe.

29. Demonstrative Pronouns

	SINGULAR				PLURAL
	M.		F.	N.	M.F.N.
NOM.	der	*he*	die	das	die
GEN.	dessen	*his*	deren	dessen	deren
DAT.	dem	*him*	der	dem	denen
ACC.	den	*him*	die	das	die

Demonstrative pronouns are emphatic forms of the personal pronouns. Emphasis is given in speech by stressing the vowel:

Sehen Sie **den Mann da?**   *Do you see that man?*
Den habe ich gefragt.   *I asked him.*
Dem glaube ich nicht.   *I don't believe him.*

30. Indefinite Pronouns

NOM.	man	*one*	jemand	*somebody,*	niemand	*nobody*
GEN.	eines		jemandes	*anybody*	niemandes	
DAT.	einem		jemand(em)		niemand(em)	
ACC.	einen		jemand(en)		niemand(en)	

a. Man is used only in the nominative; the other cases are forms of the indefinite article. **Man** is equivalent to *one, you, we, they, somebody, people,* or a passive construction:

Man nimmt oft an, daß . . .
One often assumes that . . .
Man spricht dort Deutsch.
One speaks (They / people speak) German there.
German is spoken there.
Sie sollten **einen** in Ruhe lassen.
They ought to leave one in peace.
Man sagt, daß . . .
It is said that . . .

b. Man cannot be interchanged with **er, sie,** etc.:

Wenn **man** nach Deutschland fährt, muß **man** . . .
When one goes to Germany, he must . . .

c. Jemand and **niemand** may be uninflected:

Ich habe **jemand(em)** Geld gegeben.
I gave money to somebody.
Kennen Sie **jemand(en)** in Bonn?
Do you know anybody in Bonn?
Ich habe **niemand(em)** etwas davon gesagt.
I told nobody about it.

Exercises

E.39 *Supply the correct forms of* **der, man, jemand:** (somebody)

1. _____ kenne ich, _____ können wir aber nicht fragen, er ist nicht informiert. 2. Das ist ja eine wahre Prinzessin, und mit _____ gehen Sie aus? 3. Geben Sie mir zwei Pfund von diesen Äpfeln und drei Pfund von _____ da! 4. Das sind die Brüder Weber! _deren_ Eltern habe ich noch gekannt. 5. Was für eine energische Frau! Mit _____ möchte ich keinen Streit anfangen. 6. Ist hier _Mann_, der Englisch kann? 7. Ich kenne _niemand_, der uns helfen kann. 8. Kennen Sie _____ in Ihrem

Hotel? 9. Wie kann _____ ihm glauben, wenn er immer lügt. 10. Wenn _____ kein Visum hat, lassen _____ diese Leute nicht ins Land.

E.40 *Write in German:*

1. At last we are in old Rothenburg, of which I have heard so much. 2. This is the dress I bought yesterday. 3. Lieutenant Baker, these are the soldiers who know this town. 4. That is something you will never understand. 5. I told him all I knew. 6. Where is the girl you met in Chicago? 7. With whom will you go to Europe next year? 8. Rilke, Kafka, Thomas Mann, and Brecht are the German writers whose works are known throughout the world. 9. He talks too much about himself, which I do not like. 10. That is the best I can do. 11. Whom did you ask? 12. I saw nobody when I left the office. 13. I gave your address to somebody in the office whose name I have forgotten. 14. This is the car in which he broke the record. 15. What are you waiting for? 16. He told me everything he knew.

31. Uses of sein, haben, werden

a. As Independent Verbs:

Er ist zwanzig. Er hat ein Motorrad. Es wird kalt.

b. As Helping Words:

1. **Haben** helps form the compound tenses of transitive, intransitive, and reflexive verbs, and of the modal auxiliaries:

Er **hat** einen Fasanen **geschossen.**
Es **hat** jeden Tag **geregnet.**
Er **hat** es nicht **gekonnt.**
Er **hat** gehen **müssen.**

2. **Sein** is used to form the compound tenses of intransitive verbs expressing movement to and from a place or change of state, as well as of **sein, bleiben, geschehen, gelingen:**

Sie **sind** nach Hause **gegangen.**
Er **ist** gerade von Europa **zurückgekommen.**
Es **ist** plötzlich heiß **geworden.**
Wo **bist** du **gewesen?**
Wir **sind** drei Wochen in Hamburg **geblieben.**
Was **ist geschehen?**
Es **ist** der Polizei nicht **gelungen,** ihn zu finden.

3. **Haben** is used when an intransitive verb expresses movement within a confined area:

Wir **haben** im Fluß **geschwommen.**
We had a swim in the river.
But: Wir **sind** über den Fluß **geschwommen.**
   We swam across the river.

4. **Werden** with the infinitive forms the future tenses:

Er **wird** mit dem Abendzug **kommen.**
He'll come on the evening train.

5. **Werden** with the past participle forms the passive voice (see also Section 46):

Warten Sie noch ein paar Minuten! Ihr Auto **wird** gerade **repariert.**
Wait a few minutes longer, your car is being repaired just now.

32. Summary of <u>sein</u> (to be)

PRINCIPAL PARTS: **sein, war, ist gewesen (er ist)**

INDICATIVE	SUBJUNCTIVE
	PRESENT
ich **bin**	**sei**
du **bist**	**sei(e)st**
er **ist**	**sei**
wir **sind**	**seien**
ihr **seid**	**seiet**
sie **sind**	**seien**
	PAST
ich **war**	**wäre**
du **warst**	**wärest**
er **war**	**wäre**
wir **waren**	**wären**
ihr **wart**	**wäret**
sie **waren**	**wären**
	PRESENT PERFECT
ich **bin gewesen**	**sei gewesen**
du **bist gewesen**	**seiest gewesen**
er **ist gewesen,** etc.	**sei gewesen,** etc.

PAST PERFECT

ich war gewesen   wäre gewesen
du warst gewesen   wärest gewesen
er war gewesen, etc.   wäre gewesen, etc.

FUTURE

ich werde sein   werde sein
du wirst sein   werdest sein
er wird sein, etc.   werde sein, etc.

CONDITIONAL

ich würde sein
du würdest sein
er würde sein, etc.

FUTURE PERFECT

ich werde gewesen sein   werde gewesen sein
du wirst gewesen sein, etc.   werdest gewesen sein, etc.

CONDITIONAL PERFECT

ich würde gewesen sein
du würdest gewesen sein, etc.

IMPERATIVES: familiar sing.: sei!
                                    pl.: seid!
               customary form of address: seien Sie!

33. Summary of haben (to have)

PRINCIPAL PARTS: haben, hatte, gehabt (er hat)

INDICATIVE   SUBJUNCTIVE

PRESENT

ich habe   habe
du hast   habest
er hat   habe

wir haben   haben
ihr habt   habet
sie haben   haben

PAST

ich hatte   hätte
du hattest   hättest
er hatte   hätte

wir **hatten**	**hätten**
ihr **hattet**	**hättet**
sie **hatten**	**hätten**

PRESENT PERFECT

ich **habe gehabt**	**habe gehabt**
du **hast gehabt**	**habest gehabt**
er **hat gehabt**, etc.	**habe gehabt**, etc.

PAST PERFECT

ich **hatte gehabt**	**hätte gehabt**
du **hattest gehabt**	**hättest gehabt**
er **hatte gehabt**, etc.	**hätte gehabt**, etc.

FUTURE

ich **werde haben**	**werde haben**
du **wirst haben**	**werdest haben**
er **wird haben**, etc.	**werde haben**, etc.

CONDITIONAL

ich **würde haben**
du **würdest haben**
er **würde haben**, etc.

FUTURE PERFECT

| ich **werde gehabt haben** | **werde gehabt haben** |
| du **wirst gehabt haben**, etc. | **werdest gehabt haben**, etc. |

CONDITIONAL PERFECT

ich **würde gehabt haben**
du **würdest gehabt haben**, etc.

IMPERATIVES: familiar sing.: **habe!**
pl.: **habt!**
customary form of address: **haben Sie!**

34. Summary of <u>werden</u> (to become)

PRINCIPAL PARTS: **werden, wurde, ist geworden (er wird)**

| INDICATIVE | SUBJUNCTIVE |

PRESENT

ich **werde**	**werde**
du **wirst**	**werdest**
er **wird**	**werde**

wir **werden**   **werden**
ihr **werdet**   **werdet**
sie **werden**   **werden**

PAST

ich **wurde**   **würde**
du **wurdest**   **würdest**
er **wurde**   **würde**

wir **wurden**   **würden**
ihr **wurdet**   **würdet**
sie **wurden**   **würden**

PRESENT PERFECT

ich **bin geworden**   **sei geworden**
du **bist geworden**   **seiest geworden**
er **ist geworden**, etc.   **sei geworden**, etc.

PAST PERFECT

ich **war geworden**   **wäre geworden**
du **warst geworden**   **wärest geworden**
er **war geworden**, etc.   **wäre geworden**, etc.

FUTURE

ich **werde werden**   **werde werden**
du **wirst werden**   **werdest werden**
er **wird werden**, etc.   **werde werden**, etc.

CONDITIONAL

ich **würde werden**
du **würdest werden**
er **würde werden**, etc.

FUTURE PERFECT

ich **werde geworden sein**   **werde geworden sein**
du **wirst geworden sein**, etc.   **werdest geworden sein**, etc.

CONDITIONAL PERFECT

ich **würde geworden sein**
du **würdest geworden sein**, etc.

IMPERATIVES: familiar sing.: **werde!**
                                         pl.: **werdet!**
                customary form of address: **werden Sie!**

35. Summary of Weak Verb <u>lernen</u> (to learn)

PRINCIPAL PARTS: **lernen, lernte, gelernt**

INDICATIVE	SUBJUNCTIVE

PRESENT

ich **lerne**	**lerne**
du **lernst**	**lernest**
er **lernt**	**lerne**
wir **lernen**	**lernen**
ihr **lernt**	**lernet**
sie **lernen**	**lernen**

PAST

ich **lernte**	**lernte**
du **lerntest**	**lerntest**
er **lernte**	**lernte**
wir **lernten**	**lernten**
ihr **lerntet**	**lerntet**
sie **lernten**	**lernten**

PRESENT PERFECT

ich **habe gelernt**	**habe gelernt**
du **hast gelernt**	**habest gelernt**
er **hat gelernt**, etc.	**habe gelernt**, etc.

PAST PERFECT

ich **hatte gelernt**	**hätte gelernt**
du **hattest gelernt**	**hättest gelernt**
er **hatte gelernt**, etc.	**hätte gelernt**, etc.

FUTURE

ich **werde lernen**	**werde lernen**
du **wirst lernen**	**werdest lernen**
er **wird lernen**, etc.	**werde lernen**, etc.

CONDITIONAL

ich **würde lernen**
du **würdest lernen**
er **würde lernen**, etc.

FUTURE PERFECT

| ich **werde gelernt haben** | **werde gelernt haben** |
| du **wirst gelernt haben**, etc. | **werdest gelernt haben**, etc. |

CONDITIONAL PERFECT

ich **würde gelernt haben**
du **würdest gelernt haben,** etc.

IMPERATIVES: familiar sing.: **lern(e)!** (in colloquial German
                                              without **e**)
                                      pl.: **lernt!**
                          customary form of address: **lernen Sie!**

Note: Verbs whose stems end in **-d, -t, -chn, -ckn, -dn, -fn, -gn, -tm** insert **e**
between the stem and the endings **-st** and **-t: du findest, er antwortet,
er rechnet, sie trocknet, er ordnet, du öffnest, es regnet, er atmet.**

36. Summary of Strong Verb sprechen (to speak)

PRINCIPAL PARTS: **sprechen, sprach, gesprochen (er spricht)**

INDICATIVE	SUBJUNCTIVE
	PRESENT
ich **spreche**	**spreche**
du **sprichst**	**sprechest**
er **spricht**	**spreche**
wir **sprechen**	**sprechen**
ihr **sprecht**	**sprechet**
sie **sprechen**	**sprechen**
	PAST
ich **sprach**	**spräche**
du **sprachst**	**sprächest**
er **sprach**	**spräche**
wir **sprachen**	**sprächen**
ihr **spracht**	**sprächet**
sie **sprachen**	**sprächen**
	PRESENT PERFECT
ich **habe gesprochen**	**habe gesprochen**
du **hast gesprochen**	**habest gesprochen**
er **hat gesprochen,** etc.	**habe gesprochen,** etc.

PAST PERFECT

ich **hatte gesprochen**	**hätte gesprochen**
du **hattest gesprochen**	**hättest gesprochen**
er **hatte gesprochen,** etc.	**hätte gesprochen,** etc.

FUTURE

ich **werde sprechen**	**werde sprechen**
du **wirst sprechen**	**werdest sprechen**
er **wird sprechen,** etc.	**werde sprechen,** etc.

CONDITIONAL

ich **würde sprechen**
du **würdest sprechen**
er **würde sprechen,** etc.

FUTURE PERFECT

ich **werde gesprochen haben**	**werde gesprochen haben**
du **wirst gesprochen haben,** etc.	**werdest gesprochen haben,** etc.

CONDITIONAL PERFECT

ich **würde gesprochen haben**
du **würdest gesprochen haben,** etc.

IMPERATIVES: familiar sing.: **sprich!**
                                          pl.: **sprecht!**
              customary form of address: **sprechen Sie!**

Note: 1. Strong verbs change stem vowels in the second and third persons singular:

> **a** to **ä, e** to **i(e), o** to **ö, au** to **äu: er schläft, du sprichst, er liest, er stößt, du läufst.**

2. In verbs whose stems end in **s, ß, tz,** the ending **-st** is contracted to **-t:** du **liest, läßt, sitzt.**

37. Uses of Tenses

a. Present

1. To express an action taking place at the present moment (as in English):

> Unser Mechaniker **repariert** gerade Ihr Auto.
> *Our mechanic is just now repairing your car.*

2. To express a general fact (as in English):

Unser Mechaniker **ist** nur von 9–5 in der Tankstelle.
Our mechanic is at the filling station only from 9–5.

3. To express the future in sentences containing a term of futurity, such as **morgen, bald, gleich:**

Ich **tue** es **gleich.**
I'll do it right away.

4. To express an event or a state which *has been going on* and is still going on (English progressive present perfect). In German, **schon** or **seit** is used with such statements:

Ich **warte schon lange** auf Sie.
I have been waiting a long time for you.

Note that this function of the German present tense applies only to positive statements. In negative statements the present perfect is used:

Er hat seit Sonntag nichts gegessen.
He hasn't eaten anything since Sunday.
Ich habe ihn schon lange nicht mehr gesehen.
I haven't seen him for a long time.

b. Past

1. To express past events in narrative style (as in English):

Wir **fuhren** in die Stadt, **kauften** einen Mantel und **aßen** zu Mittag.
We drove to town, bought an overcoat, and had lunch.

2. To express, together with **seit** or **schon,** an event or a state which *had been going on* and was still going on (English progressive past perfect):

Er spielte seit zwei Stunden Klavier.
He had been playing the piano *for two hours.*
Er wartete schon eine Stunde.
He had been waiting for an hour.

c. Present Perfect (also called Compound Past)

1. To express isolated events in the recent past (English simple past):

Ich **habe** ihm gestern **geschrieben.**
I wrote him yesterday.

2. To express an event that will have taken place at a stated time:

Ich habe das Stück **bis morgen** zu Ende **gelesen.**
I will have finished reading the play by tomorrow.

d. Past Perfect

To express an event or state which already was concluded when something else happened (as in English):

Ich **hatte** gerade meinen Brief **beendet,** als er ins Zimmer trat.
I had just finished my letter when he entered the room.

e. Future

1. To express an event or state in the future (as in English):

Ich **werde** dir **helfen.**
I will help you.

2. To denote, with **wohl,** probability in the present (English present tense):

Das Licht ist an. Er **wird wohl** zu Hause **sein.**
The light is on. He is probably at home.

f. Future Perfect

To express, with **wohl,** probability in the past (English past or present perfect):

Das Licht ist aus. Er **wird wohl** das Haus **verlassen haben.**
The light is out. He probably left the house.

g. Conditional

To express an unreal condition:

Ich **würde** ihn **verstehen,** wenn er lauter **sprechen würde** (spräche).
I would understand him, if he would speak louder.

h. Conditional Perfect

To express an unreal condition in the past. This form is normally replaced by the past perfect subjunctive (past subjunctive II):

Ich **hätte** ihn besser **verstanden.**
Instead of: Ich **würde** ihn besser **verstanden haben.**
I would have understood him better.

Exercises

E.41 *Express in German:*

1. He tells me nothing. 2. She is driving to Berlin. 3. Does your father

always open the door? 4. Who is coming? 5. Does he know her? 6. I
am smiling, but he is not smiling. 7. I have been in Cologne for a year.
8. How long have you been here? 9. He has been working for months.
10. We have known each other for a long time. 11. They have been
living in that house for two years. 12. She has been studying for a long
time. 13. We have been in Hamburg for two days. 14. Will she come
tomorrow? 15. Next summer I will go to Germany. 16. When are you
going there? 17. I will not do that. 18. When will you come back?
19. Tomorrow I am going to the opera. 20. Who will answer the question?

38. Strong Verbs (Ablaut Classes)

Ablaut denotes change of stem vowel (*sing, sang, sung*). Grouping frequent
German verbs according to Ablaut Classes will help you become more
familiar with the various vowel changes and derive the principal parts to
verbs with prefixes, such as **schreiben, schrieb, geschrieben** and **beschreiben,
beschrieb, beschrieben.**

CLASS IA

bleiben	blieb	ist geblieben	*remain, stay*
scheinen	schien	geschienen	*shine; seem*
schreiben	schrieb	geschrieben	*write*
schreien	schrie	geschrie(e)n	*shout, shriek*
schweigen	schwieg	geschwiegen	*be silent*
steigen	stieg	ist gestiegen	*climb, rise*
verzeihen	verzieh	verziehen	*pardon*

CLASS IB

leiden	litt	gelitten	*suffer*
pfeifen	pfiff	gepfiffen	*whistle*
reiten	ritt	(ist) geritten	*ride (an animal)*
schneiden	schnitt	geschnitten	*cut*
zerreißen	zerriß	zerrissen	*tear up*

CLASS IIA

biegen	bog	gebogen	*bend, turn*
bieten	bot	geboten	*offer, bid*
fliegen	flog	ist geflogen	*fly*
fliehen	floh	ist geflohen	*flee*
frieren	fror	gefroren	*freeze, be cold*
lügen	log	gelogen	*tell lies*

schieben	schob	geschoben	*shove, push*
verbieten	verbot	verboten	*forbid*
verlieren	verlor	verloren	*lose*
wiegen	wog	gewogen	*weigh*
ziehen	zog	(ist) gezogen	*pull; move; go*

CLASS IIB

fließen	floß	ist geflossen	*flow*
riechen	roch	gerochen	*smell*
schießen	schoß	geschossen	*shoot*
schließen	schloß	geschlossen	*close; conclude*

to perceive odor or to give off " ? (handwritten note)

CLASS IIIA

binden	band	gebunden	*tie*
finden	fand	gefunden	*find*
gelingen	gelang	ist gelungen	*succeed*
singen	sang	gesungen	*sing*
sinken	sank	ist gesunken	*sink*
springen	sprang	ist gesprungen	*jump*
trinken	trank	getrunken	*drink*
verschwinden	verschwand	ist verschwunden	*disappear*

CLASS IIIB

beginnen	begann	begonnen	*begin*
gewinnen	gewann	gewonnen	*win, gain*
schwimmen	schwamm	(ist) geschwommen	*swim*

CLASS IV

befehlen	befahl	befohlen	er befiehlt	*order*
brechen	brach	gebrochen	er bricht	*break*
gelten	galt	gegolten	er gilt	*be worth, valid*
helfen	half	geholfen	er hilft	*help*
nehmen	nahm	genommen	er nimmt	*take*
sprechen	sprach	gesprochen	er spricht	*speak*
stehlen	stahl	gestohlen	er stiehlt	*steal*
sterben	starb	ist gestorben	er stirbt	*die*
treffen	traf	getroffen	er trifft	*meet; hit*
werfen	warf	geworfen	er wirft	*throw*

CLASS V

essen	aß	gegessen	er ißt	*eat*
geben	gab	gegeben	er gibt	*give*
geschehen	geschah	ist geschehen	es geschieht	*happen*
lesen	las	gelesen	er liest	*read*
sehen	sah	gesehen	er sieht	*see*

treten	trat	(ist) getreten	er tritt	*step; kick*
vergessen	vergaß	vergessen	er vergißt	*forget*

CLASS VI

einladen	lud ein	eingeladen	er lädt ein	*invite*
erfahren	erfuhr	erfahren	er erfährt	*find out*
fahren	fuhr	(ist) gefahren	er fährt	*go; drive*
graben	grub	gegraben	er gräbt	*dig*
schlagen	schlug	geschlagen	er schlägt	*beat, strike*
tragen	trug	getragen	er trägt	*carry; wear*
wachsen	wuchs	ist gewachsen	er wächst	*grow*
waschen	wusch	gewaschen	er wäscht	*wash*

CLASS VIIA

fallen	fiel	ist gefallen	er fällt	*fall*
halten	hielt	gehalten	er hält	*hold; stop*
heißen	hieß	geheißen	er heißt	*be called*
lassen	ließ	gelassen	er läßt	*let, leave (behind)*
laufen	lief	ist gelaufen	er läuft	*run*
raten	riet	geraten	er rät	*advise; guess*
rufen	rief	gerufen	er ruft	*call*
schlafen	schlief	geschlafen	er schläft	*sleep*
stoßen	stieß	gestoßen	er stößt	*push; stumble on*

CLASS VIIB

anfangen	fing an	angefangen	er fängt an	*begin*

IRREGULAR STRONG VERBS

bitten	bat	gebeten		*ask, request*
gehen	ging	ist gegangen		*go, walk*
heben	hob	gehoben		*raise, lift*
kommen	kam	ist gekommen		*come*
liegen	lag	(ist) gelegen		*lie; be situated*
sein	war	ist gewesen	er ist	*be*
sitzen	saß	gesessen		*sit*
stehen	stand	gestanden		*stand*
tun	tat	getan		*do*
werden	wurde	ist geworden	er wird	*become*

IRREGULAR WEAK VERBS

brennen	brannte	gebrannt		*burn*
bringen	brachte	gebracht		*bring, take*
denken	dachte	gedacht		*think*
haben	hatte	gehabt	er hat	*have*

kennen	kannte	gekannt		*know* (persons or things)
nennen	nannte	genannt		*name, call*
rennen	rannte	ist gerannt		*run*
senden	sandte	gesandt		*send*
wenden	wandte	gewandt		*turn*
wissen	wußte	gewußt	er **weiß**	*know* (facts)

Exercises

E.42 *Supply the correct form of the verb in parentheses, which may appear as an infinitive, a present or past tense form, a past participle, or an imperative. Imperatives are followed by an exclamation point. If both the present or past tense fit, use both tenses:*

EXAMPLES:

Hast du mit ihm _____ (sprich!)?   Hast du mit ihm gesprochen?
_____ langsamer! (gefahren)   Fahr langsamer!
Er _____ ins Haus. (er geht)   Er ging ins Haus.
Er _____ noch im Bett. (gelegen)   Er liegt noch im Bett. Er lag noch
                                                                      im Bett.

[Divisions of (3)]   idiom

1. Wer hat den Lohengrin _____? (sang) 2. Er hat sich in den Finger _____. (er schneidet) 3. Er _____ den Brief. (er zerreißt) 4. Selbst die stärksten Bäume _____ sich im Sturm. (biegen) 5. Hat der erste Akt schon _____? (beginnen) 6. Hast du gut _____? (schlief) 7. _____ lauter, Gerhard! (er sprach) 8. Viel Blut ist _____. (fließen) 9. Hast du die Tür _____ (schließ!) 10. Er hat mir nicht genug _____. (er bietet) 11. Der Wind _____ wie ein Messer. (er schneidet) 12. Du _____ nicht genug. (aß) 13. Hast du ihm ein Trinkgeld _____? (gib!) 14. Was ist _____? (es geschieht) 15. _____ mal die Zeitung! (las) 16. Er _____ nichts davon. (er wußte) 17. Ich bin die ganze Zeit _____. (er lief) 18. Sie _____ heute ihr neues Kleid. (er trug) 19. _____ dir die Hände! (er wusch) 20. Wer hat ihn _____? (er lud ein) 21. Er _____ eine Weile. (er schweigt) 22. Er _____ sich besser zu fühlen. (scheinen) 23. Das Baby _____. (geschrieen) 24. Sie hat ihm _____. (verzeih!) 25. Martha, _____ mir noch dies eine Mal! (er half) 26. _____ eine Taxe, Herr Kröger! (nimm!) 27. Er _____ den Diskus über 50 m. (geworfen) 28. Der Kriegsgefangene wurde _____ ins Lager gebracht. (er band) 29. Wo hast du das _____? (er findet) 30. Wer hat hier _____? (er schießt) 31. Er _____ auf dem Operationstisch. (er stirbt) 32. _____ Sie nicht! (er log) 33. _____ das Boot aus dem

Wasser, Jungens! (gezogen) 34. Das Schiff ist hier in der Nähe _____.
(es sinkt) 35. Der Bär _____ sechshundert Pfund. (gewogen). 36. Wir
_____ uns vor dem Kaffee Kranzler. (er trifft) 37. Wer _____ hier?
(er befahl) 38. _____ später! (er kam) 39. Der Feind ist _____. (er
schlug) 40. Niemand _____ das. (gesehen) 41. Wer hier _____, findet
nichts. (er grub) 42. Er _____ oft um Geld. (gebeten) 43. Hat die Oper
schon _____? (er fängt an) 44. Er _____ mir, zu einem anderen Arzt
zu gehen. (geraten) 45. Wer hat das _____? (tun) 46. Es ist kalt _____.
(es wurde) 47. Er _____ uns Geld aus Amerika. (gesandt) 48. Er
hatte nichts. (gehabt) 49. Es _riecht_ nach gutem Essen. (rieche!)
50. Rauchen ist _verboten_. (verbieten) 51. Es _gelingt_ ihm, reich zu heiraten.
(gelungen) 52. Wieder hat unsere Mannschaft nicht _gewonnen_. (er gewann)
53. Warum haben Sie meinen Hund _getreten_? (er tritt) 54. Hier _stand_
vor dem Kriege ein Denkmal. (gestanden) 55. Er _riet_ uns, erst nach
München zu fahren. (geraten) 56. Wer hat mich _gerufen_? (er rief)
57. Er war schon _gegangen_ (geh!) 58. _Hebt_ nicht zuviel! (er hob)
59. Der Frühling ist _gekommen_. (er kam) 60. Bonn _liegt_ am Rhein. (er
lag) 61. _Hält_ dieser Zug in Lüneburg? (gehalten) 62. _Brich_ dir nicht
das Bein! (gebrochen) 63. Wieviel _gilt_ ein amerikanischer Dollar
hier? (gegolten) 64. Die Sonne ist _gesunken_. Es ist Zeit zu gehen. (er sank)
65. Dies sind die _gestohlen_ Diamanten. (er stahl) 66. Wir haben das Auto
eine halbe Stunde lang _geschoben_. (schieben) 67. _Weiß_ sie es? (gewußt)
68. Damals _sandte_ er viele Care-Pakete nach Deutschland. (senden)
69. Nero _sang_, als Rom _brannte_. (gesungen) (brennen) 70. _Bringe_
mich nach Hause! Ich bin müde, Bruno. (gebracht) 71. Ich _dachte_,
heute wäre Sonnabend. (denken) 72. Du wirst dein ganzes Geld _verlieren_
(verloren) 73. Ich _fror_ unter der leichten Decke. (frieren) 74. Die
übrigen Flugzeuge _floh_. (flieh!) 75. Wie lange seid ihr in München
geblieben? (bleibt!) 76. König Gustav Adolf _ritt_ auf einem Schimmel
in seine letzte Schlacht. (er reitet) 77. Der Wind _pfiff_ uns um die
Ohren. (gepfiffen) 78. _Vergiß_ mich nicht! (vergessen) 79. _Seid_ ruhig,
Jungens! Es ist schon Mitternacht. (er war) 80. Es war uns zu kalt. Wir
sind nach Hause _gegangen_. (er ging) 81. Anstatt schwimmen zu gehen,
haben sie die ganze Zeit im Kino _gesessen_. (er saß) 82. Als ich das hörte,
bin ich sofort nach Hause _gerannt_. (er rennt) 83. Er _ließ_ vor Schreck
die Tasse fallen. (er läßt) 84. Wir _flogen_ mit der Lufthansa. (er fliegt)
85. Ich _erfuhr_ von seinen Verwandten, daß er nach Amerika ausge-
wandert ist. (erfahren) 86. So ein Baum _wächst_ auch in meinem Garten.
(gewachsen) 87. Der erste Schnee _fällt_; der Winter ist _gekommen_. (er fiel)
(er kam) 88. Damals _hießen_ sie noch Willmers. Sie hat dann Herrn
Behrend geheiratet. (heißen) 89. Was _liest_ du da? (gelesen) 90. Man
nannte diesen Fußballspieler den „fliegenden Holländer". (genannt)

39. Modal Auxiliaries

Six verbs, known as Modal Auxiliaries, express mood or attitude, rather than a specific state or action. These verbs have many meanings.

a. dürfen

(expressing permission) *may, be permitted to, be allowed to;* (in a negative sentence in the present tense) *must not*

Er **darf rauchen.**
He may (is permitted to, is allowed to) smoke.
Er **darf nicht rauchen.**
He may not (must not, is not allowed to) smoke.
Er **hat nicht rauchen dürfen.**
He was not permitted to (allowed to) smoke.

b. können

(expressing ability and possibility) *can, be able to; may*

Ich **kann** die Frage **beantworten.**
I can (am able to) answer the question.
Du **kannst gehen.**
You may (can) go.
Das **kann sein.**
That may be.
Er **kann** es **gesagt haben.**
He may have said it.
Er **kann Deutsch.**
He knows German. (He can speak, read, etc., German.)
Er **hat nicht kommen können.**
He has not been able to (could not) come.
Sie **hätten** ihn **warnen können.**
You could have warned him.

c. mögen

(expressing liking or preference) *like to;* (expressing possibility or probability) *may;* (the subjunctive form **möchte**) *would like to*

Er **mag** München am liebsten.
He likes Munich best.
Ich **mag** sie.
I like her.
Das **hätte** ich **sehen mögen.**
I should have liked to see that.

Er **mochte** 5 Jahre alt sein.
He may have been (was perhaps) 5 years old.
Möchten Sie sonst noch etwas?
Would you like anything else?

d. müssen

(expressing necessity and compulsion) *must, have to*

Ich **muß** in die Stadt **gehen.**
I must (have to) go to town.
Er **mußte** lauter **sprechen.**
He had to talk louder.

e. sollen

(expressing obligation and expectation) *be supposed to; should, ought*

Sie **sollen** pünktlich **sein.**
You are supposed to be on time.
Er **soll** sehr reich **sein.**
He is supposed to (said to) be very rich.
Er **sollte** die Rechnung **bezahlen.**
He was supposed to pay the bill.
Er **sollte sich beeilen.**
He should (ought to) hurry.
Er **hätte** das **nicht tun sollen.**
He should not have done that.

f. wollen

(expressing desire and wish) *want to, intend to; claim to*

Willst du gehen?
Do you want to go?
Er **will** den Brief **nicht schreiben.**
He doesn't want to (refuses to) write the letter.
Er **will** morgen **abfahren.**
He intends to leave tomorrow.
Er **will** alles besser **wissen.**
He claims to know everything better.

40. Principal Parts of Modals

INF.	PRES.	PAST	PAST PARTICIPLE	
			1	2
können	kann	konnte	gekonnt	können

INF.	PRES.	PAST	PAST PARTICIPLE	
			1	2
mögen	mag	mochte	gemocht	mögen
müssen	muß	mußte	gemußt	müssen
dürfen	darf	durfte	gedurft	dürfen
wollen	will	wollte	gewollt	wollen
sollen	soll	sollte	gesollt	sollen

41. Conjugation of Modals

a. Present Tense

	können	mögen	müssen	dürfen	wollen	sollen
ich	kann	mag	muß	darf	will	soll
du	kannst	magst	mußt	darfst	willst	sollst
er	kann	mag	muß	darf	will	soll
wir	können	mögen	müssen	dürfen	wollen	sollen
ihr	könnt	mögt	müßt	dürft	wollt	sollt
sie	können	mögen	müssen	dürfen	wollen	sollen
Sie	können	mögen	müssen	dürfen	wollen	sollen

Note: 1. Modal auxiliaries have no endings in the first and third persons singular: Ich **muß** jetzt nach Hause gehen.

2. The dependent infinitives **gehen** and **tun** are often omitted:

Ich **muß** um elf nach Hause.
I have to go home at eleven.
Der Verkehr war so stark, wir **konnten nicht** über die Straße.
The traffic was so heavy, we could not cross (go across) the street.

3. Instead of repeating a verb after the modal auxiliary, English simply uses "to," which is left from "to do that":

Why did you not help him? *I was not able to.*

German frequently uses **es** instead of repeating the infinitive:

Warum hast du ihm nicht geholfen? Ich **konnte es nicht.**
But also: Ich **konnte nicht.**

b. Past Tense

The past tense of modals is formed like the past tense of weak verbs. Drop the umlaut and add the tense sign **-t-** and the personal endings to the stem:

können	ich **konnte**	*I was able to*
mögen	ich **mochte**	*I liked to*
dürfen	ich **durfte**	*I was permitted to*
müssen	ich **mußte**	*I had to*
sollen	ich **sollte**	*I was supposed to, I was to*
wollen	ich **wollte**	*I wanted to*

c. Present and Past Perfect

The modal auxiliaries use **haben** for the formation of compound tenses: the present perfect and past perfect. They have two forms for the past participle (see 40). The regular form (**gekonnt, gemußt,** etc.) is used when a dependent infinitive is not expressed. The form identical with the infinitive (**können, müssen,** etc.) is used when a dependent infinitive is expressed:

Er **hat es gemußt.**	*He (has) had to.*
Er **hat es tun müssen.**	*He (has) had to do it.*
Er **hat es nicht gedurft.**	*He wasn't permitted to.*
Er **hat nicht gehen dürfen.**	*He was not permitted to go.*

d. Future

The future of a modal auxiliary ends with a double infinitive:

Ich werde ihr alles **sagen müssen.**

This double infinitive, a "block of verbs," also stands at the end of the clause in dependent word order:

Es tut mir leid, daß ich ihr alles **werde sagen müssen.**

The same rule prevails in the present and past perfect:

Es tut mir leid, daß ich ihr alles **habe sagen müssen.**

Exercises

E.43 *Change the following sentences to (a) simple past; (b) present perfect; and (c) translate into English:*

1. Er muß schwer arbeiten. 2. Er kann das Zigarettenrauchen nicht aufgeben. 3. Bei dieser Arbeit kann mir keiner helfen. 4. Wir dürfen dieses Paket nicht nach Ostdeutschland schicken. 5. Erich soll den Kartoffelsalat zum Picknick mitbringen. 6. Ruth will nicht in seinem Auto mitfahren.

E.44 *Change the plural subjects and verb forms to the corresponding singular forms:*

1. Wir müssen morgen in die Stadt fahren. 2. Wie können sie das alles wissen? 3. Ihr dürft jetzt gehen. 4. Die Ärzte können ihm nicht helfen. 5. Wann wollt ihr nach Hause kommen? 6. Die jungen Mädchen mögen ihn. 7. Was wollen die Beamten von mir? Alle Passagiere sollen ihre Pässe zeigen. 8. Sie können nicht lauter sprechen. 9. Wir können dich nicht jeden Tag besuchen. 10. Was wollt ihr von mir?

42. Hören, Sehen, Lassen

Like the modals, these verbs combine with another infinitive without **zu,** thus forming a "block":

Has du sie **singen hören?**
Did you hear her sing?
Ich habe ihn **fallen sehen.**
I saw him fall(ing).
Wissen Sie, warum er ihn nicht **hat gehen lassen?**
Do you know why he did not let him go?

43. Wissen

The verb **wissen (weiß, wußte, gewußt)** is not a modal auxiliary but is conjugated like one; that is, it has no endings in the first and third persons singular; the infinitive vowel occurs in the plural:

PRESENT	PAST
ich **weiß**	ich **wußte**
du **weißt**	du **wußtest**
er **weiß**	er **wußte**
wir **wissen**	wir **wußten**
ihr **wißt**	ihr **wußtet**
sie **wissen**	sie **wußten**
Sie **wissen**	Sie **wußten**

Exercise

prepare a (3-5) minute speech in German

E.45 *Express in German:* (WRITE OUT)

1. Must you go? 2. We are not supposed to see him before tomorrow.

3. Do you really want to see that picture? 4. Can you give me his telephone number? 5. He had to drive to Würzburg. 6. I know that he has never wanted to travel through Europe. 7. He will not be allowed to get up; he is still too weak. 8. What did she want? 9. You know that I may not swim in such cold water. 10. Have you forgotten what you must still do today? 11. I have no money. I can't go to the movies. 12. Why don't you work on Saturday? I am not permitted to. 13. Why don't you leave him in Berlin? —I can't do that. —You can't do that or you are not permitted to? 14. Did you not know that he had to work last Saturday? 15. You won't be able to help him. 16. I know that he had always wanted to see the U.S.A. 17. When must you go home? 18. Did you not hear me come? 19. Did you leave your handbag (lying) in the subway? 20. The great writers and philosophers have seen all that coming. 21. Did you know (have you known) that I had to (had had to) pay the bill?

44. Compound Verbs

Many German verbs are compounded with a prefix.

a. Separable Prefixes

Such prefixes are usually adverbs with a meaning of their own. They bear the main stress and are separated from the verb in the present, past, and imperative, standing last in the clause:

Ich **stehe** jeden Morgen um 7 Uhr **auf.**
I get up every morning at 7 o'clock.
Ich **stand** jeden Morgen um 7 Uhr **auf.**
I got up every morning at 7 o'clock.
Stehen Sie um 7 Uhr **auf!**
Get up at 7 o'clock.

In the present perfect and past perfect, the prefix is attached to the past participle:

Ich **bin** früh **aufgestanden.**
I got up early.
Ich **war** früh **aufgestanden.**
I had gotten up early.

When the infinitive form is used with **zu, zu** stands between the prefix and the infinitive, and the three parts are one word:

Es war mir unmöglich, so früh **aufzustehen.**
It was impossible for me to get up so early.

The principal parts of a verb with separable prefix are given in the following way:

aufstehen, stand auf, ist aufgestanden
sich anziehen, zog sich an, sich angezogen

b. Inseparable Prefixes

1. The inseparable prefixes are: **be-, emp-, ent-, er-, ge-, miß-, ver-, zer-.** They are not stressed, there is no **ge-** in the past participle, and **zu** of the infinitive construction is not inserted between the prefix and the verb:

Das **erklärt** alles.
That explains everything.
Das **erklärte** alles.
That explained everything.
Erklären Sie alles!
Explain everything.
Er hat alles **erklärt.**
He has explained everything.
Wir haben ihn gebeten, alles **zu erklären.**
We have asked him to explain everything.

2. Certain separable prefixes are inseparable with verbs having special meanings. Common examples of such inseparable verbs are:

überfahren	*to run over*	**sich unterhalten**	*to converse*
überreden	*to persuade*	**unterrichten**	*to teach*
überraschen	*to surprise*	**unterscheiden**	*to distinguish*
übersetzen	*to translate*	**untersuchen**	*to investigate*
übertreiben	*to exaggerate*	**widersprechen**	*to contradict*
überzeugen	*to convince*	**widerstehen**	*to resist*
umgeben	*to surround*	**wiederholen**	*to repeat*
unterbrechen	*to interrupt*		

Exercises

E.46 *Restate the following sentences by dropping the modal auxiliary. Retain the same tense:*

EXAMPLE: Er wollte nicht mitkommen.
Er kam nicht mit.

1. Sie kann um acht Uhr anfangen. 2. Wir wollen heute schon fortfahren. 3. Du sollst um sechs Uhr aufstehen. 4. Er will diesen Film in

Deutschland einführen. 5. Sie dürfen Ihren Bruder mitbringen. 6. Ich muß mich auf das Examen vorbereiten. 7. Sie wollte mit Peter ausgehen.

E.47 *Restate the sentences in E.46 without modal auxiliary, using the present perfect tense.*

E.48 *Give the three command forms for each of the following:*

EXAMPLE: aufhören: Hör auf! Hört auf! Hören Sie auf!

1. aufstehen.   2. anfangen.   3. mitkommen.   4. sich vorbereiten.
5. die Tür zumachen.

E.49 *Combine the two sentences by making an infinitive phrase of the second:*

EXAMPLE: Ich habe keine Lust. Ich will nicht mitgehen.
             Ich habe keine Lust mitzugehen.

1. Es ist mir nicht möglich. Ich kann nicht früher aufstehen. 2. Ist es uns erlaubt? Wir wollen jetzt fortgehen. 3. Ich habe keine Zeit. Ich will jetzt nicht anfangen. 4. Es ist mir unmöglich. Ich mag nicht mit diesem Menschen ausgehen.

45. Passive Voice

a. In the active voice, the subject of the sentence "acts":

Das Flugzeug entdeckte das Unterseeboot.
The plane discovered the submarine.

In the passive voice, the subject "is acted upon," hence is passive:

Das Unterseeboot wurde von dem Flugzeug **entdeckt.**
The submarine was discovered by the plane.

English expresses the passive voice by the auxiliary *to be* plus past participle; German uses **werden** plus past participle.

b. The direct object of the active construction becomes the subject of the passive construction:

Das Flugzeug entdeckte **das Unterseeboot.**
Das Unterseeboot wurde von dem Flugzeug entdeckt.

c. The indirect object is not affected when a sentence is changed to the passive:

Sie hilft **ihm** oft.
Ihm wird oft von ihr geholfen.

d. The preposition *by* introduces the agent in an English passive construction. In German two different prepositions are used, although this differentiation is not strictly adhered to:

von introduces the agent:

Das Unterseeboot wurde **von einem Flieger** gesichtet.
The submarine was sighted by a pilot.

durch introduces the means:

Die Stadt wurde **durch (von) Bomben** zerstört.
The city was destroyed by bombs.

46. Forms of the Passive

Der Wagen **wird repariert.**	*The car is being repaired.*
Der Wagen **wurde repariert.**	*The car was repaired.*
Der Wagen **ist repariert worden.**	*The car has been (was) repaired.*
Der Wagen **war repariert worden.**	*The car had been repaired.*
Der Wagen **wird repariert werden.**	*The car will be repaired.*

Note: **Werden** is inflected regularly; its past participle, however, is **worden.**

47. Uses of the Passive

a. The meaning of a statement in either the active or the passive voice is generally the same. Using one or the other is a matter of style. The passive is preferred if the agent of an action is not specified:

Diese alten Lieder werden oft gesungen.
These old songs are sung often.
Über diesen Fall ist viel geschrieben worden.
Much has been written about this case.

b. Impersonal Passive

In some passive constructions, no person or thing being acted upon is expressed:

Es wurde viel **getanzt.**   *There was a lot of dancing.*
Es wurde viel **gelacht.**   *There was much laughing.*

c. Modals and the Passive Infinitive

Observe the two infinitives used with the modal auxiliary:

Dr. Carlson mußte **operieren.**	*Dr. Carlson had to operate.*
Dr. Carlson mußte **operiert werden.**	*Dr. Carlson had to be operated on.*

Operieren is the active infinitive and **operiert werden** the passive infinitive. The passive infinitive consists of the past participle of the verb and the infinitive of **werden.**

48. Contrast between Action and State

Die Karten **werden** hier **verkauft.**	*The tickets are being sold here.*
Die Karten **sind verkauft.**	*The tickets are sold.*

The first sentence expresses an action; **werden verkauft** is passive. The second sentence expresses a state; **verkauft** is a predicate adjective, like **teuer** in the sentence: **Die Karten sind teuer.** *The tickets are expensive.*

Exercises

E.50 *Change the following sentences to the passive voice, keeping the tense of the original:*

1. In Deutschland spült der Gast nie das Geschirr. 2. Die Zuschauer feierten den Sieg der Fußballmannschaft. 3. Die Deutschen haben viele amerikanische Wörter in ihre Sprache aufgenommen. 4. Die Technik bietet der modernen Hausfrau viel. 5. Ausländer verstehen selten das amerikanische Fußballspiel. 6. Dieses Volksfest drückt den amerikanischen Nationalcharakter aus. 7. Ein sehr guter Schauspieler hatte die Hauptrolle gespielt. 8. Die Schlepper ziehen jetzt den Ozeandampfer vom Pier weg. 9. Das Artilleriefeuer störte den schlafenden Soldaten nicht. 10. Welche Themen besprechen Ihre Professoren in ihren Vorlesungen? 11. Die ganze Klasse wird große Fortschritte machen. 12. Der Assistent mußte das Experiment genau beschreiben. 13. Man soll neugelernte Wörter immer aufschreiben.

E.51 *Express in German:*

1. Good jokes are often heard in this café. 2. My car had been repaired by the mechanic. 3. I don't want to be disturbed by this noise. 4. Students will always be criticized by miserly landladies. 5. The library was

closed all summer.   6. No apples tonight. They are all sold.   7. Apples
were being sold in the street, and I bought a pound.   8. Much can be
learned in a café discussion.   9. The tickets were punched by the conductor.   10. The parking lot was closed last night, but it will be opened
at nine o'clock this morning.   11. The noise of the market place cannot
be heard through these thick walls.   12. The game was lost in the last
minute.   13. His novel will be praised by all critics.   14. The purpose of
the test was not understood by the students.   15. Many important political questions had been discussed in these lectures.

E.52 *Translate the following sentences and note the three functions of* **werden:**

1. Der junge Mann wurde Soldat.   2. Diese Theorie kann nicht von
allen verstanden werden.   3. Es wird ihm klar werden.   4. Zeitungen
werden im Bahnhof verkauft.   5. Heute wird getanzt.   6. Wir wurden
in den Speisesaal gerufen.   7. Es wird heller.   8. Schiller wurde im Jahre
1759 geboren.   9. Wirst du länger in Wien bleiben?   10. Die Tür wird
um 10 Uhr geschlossen.   11. Seid ihr alle müde geworden?   12. Sie ist
ein wenig melancholisch geworden.   13. Es begann, dunkel zu werden.
14. Du wirst dick werden, wenn du immer so viel ißt.   15. Der Dom ist
im 16. Jahrhundert gebaut worden.

49. Subjunctive

a. Formation

1. The endings for all tenses of the subjunctive are the same for all verbs,
   except the first and third persons singular present of **sein** (ich **sei,** er
   sei): -e, -est, -e, -en, -et, -en.

2. The Present Subjunctive (also called Present Subjunctive I) is formed
   by adding the endings to the infinitive stem. The irregularities that
   exist in the present indicative of certain verbs (er **hat, spricht, kann**)
   do not occur in the subjunctive:

	spielen	haben	schreiben	sprechen	sein	können
ich	spiele	habe	schreibe	spreche	sei	könne
du	spielest	habest	schreibest	sprechest	sei(e)st	könnest
er	spiele	habe	schreibe	spreche	sei	könne
wir	spielen	haben	schreiben	sprechen	seien	können
ihr	spielet	habet	schreibet	sprechet	seiet	könnet
sie	spielen	haben	schreiben	sprechen	seien	können

3. The Past Subjunctive (also called Present Subjunctive II) is formed
by adding the subjunctive endings to the past stem. Strong verbs with
a vowel that can be modified, as well as **haben** and the modal auxiliaries
(except **sollen** and **wollen**), take an umlaut:

WEAK	STRONG		IRREGULAR		MODAL
spielte	schrieb	sprach	war	hatte	konnte
ich **spielte**	schriebe	spräche	wäre	hätte	könnte
du **spieltest**	schriebest	sprächest	wärest	hättest	könntest
er **spielte**	schriebe	spräche	wäre	hätte	könnte
wir **spielten**	schrieben	sprächen	wären	hätten	könnten
ihr **spieltet**	schriebet	sprächet	wäret	hättet	könntet
sie **spielten**	schrieben	sprächen	wären	hätten	könnten

Note the irregular forms: er **stürbe, hülfe, würfe.**

4. The six irregular verbs **brennen, kennen, nennen, rennen, senden,
wenden** do not take the umlaut in the past subjunctive:

wenn es **brennte,** wenn er mich **kennte,** wenn er sie **nennte,** wenn er es
sendete, wenn er das Auto **wendete.**

5. The Present Perfect Subjunctive (also called Past Subjunctive I) and
the Past Perfect Subjunctive (also called Past Subjunctive II) consist
of the present and past subjunctives of **haben** and **sein** plus past
participle:

PRES. PERF. SUBJ.	PAST PERF. SUBJ.
er **habe gespielt**	er **hätte gespielt**
er **sei gekommen**	er **wäre gekommen**
er **sei gewesen**	er **wäre gewesen**
er **habe gehabt**	er **hätte gehabt**

6. The Future Tenses and the Conditionals are formed by the present
or past subjunctive of **werden** plus present or perfect infinitive:

FUTURE SUBJ.	CONDITIONAL
er **werde** spielen	er **würde** spielen
er **werde** sein	er **würde** sein

FUTURE PERF. SUBJ.	CONDITIONAL PERFECT
er **werde gespielt haben**	er **würde gespielt haben**
er **werde gewesen sein**	er **würde gewesen sein**

b. Conditions and Wishes

1. Time Reference: Present and Future

German and English use the past subjunctive to express a condition contrary to fact as it exists at the present time and in the future. The conclusion is expressed in English by *would* plus infinitive (*I would write*). German may use either the subjunctive (**schriebe**) or, preferably, the auxiliary **würde** plus infinitive (**würde schreiben**), unless the verb in the conclusion is either **haben, sein, werden,** or a modal auxiliary.

Condition:

Wenn ich Zeit **hätte, würde** ich ihm **schreiben** (**schriebe** ich ihm).
If I had the time, I would write him.
Wenn er nicht so stolz **wäre, könnte** man ihm helfen.
If he were not so proud, one could help him.

Wish:

Wenn ich nur mehr Zeit **hätte!**
If only I had more time.
Ich wünschte, ich **hätte** mehr Zeit.
I wish I had more time.

2. Time Reference: Past

The past perfect subjunctive expresses a condition contrary to fact in the past. In the conclusion, the same construction is used, because the form with **würde** (**würde geschrieben haben**) is too cumbersome.

Condition:

Wenn ich Zeit **gehabt hätte, hätte** ich ihm **geschrieben.**
If I had had the time, I would have written him.
Wenn es nicht so kalt **gewesen wäre, wäre** ich **mitgegangen.**
If it had not been so cold, I would have gone along.

Wish:

Ich wünschte, ich **hätte** mehr Zeit **gehabt.**
I wish I had had more time.
Ich wünschte, es **wäre** nicht so kalt **gewesen.**
I wish it had not been so cold.

3. Omission of **wenn**

To express the condition, **wenn** may be omitted and inverted word order used. The main clause is usually introduced by **so:**

Hätte ich mehr Zeit **gehabt,** so **hätte** ich ihm **geschrieben.**

4. Condition not expressed

A statement can indirectly imply a condition:

REFERRING TO PRESENT: Das **wäre** möglich.
That would be possible.

REFERRING TO PAST: Das **wäre** möglich **gewesen.**
That would have been possible.

c. Indirect Discourse

1. Indirect discourse is a form of expression in which the substance of a statement of another person is related without being quoted. Statement: *"I am ill";* quoted: *John said: "I am ill";* expressed indirectly: *John said he was ill.*

German differs from English in two important points:

(a) German verbs in indirect discourse are in the subjunctive; English rarely uses subjunctive forms in indirect discourse.
(b) The tense of the introductory verb has no influence on the tense of the verb in indirect discourse; in English it does (he *says* he *is;* he *said* he *was*).

Indirect discourse usually occurs after verbs of saying and thinking, such as **sagen, erzählen, denken, glauben fragen, hoffen, schreiben,** and others.

2. In expressing a direct statement indirectly, the following changes in tense and mood of the verbs occur:

(a) Present Indicative   becomes Present or Past Subj.
(b) Past, Pres. Perf., Past Perf. become Present or Past Perf. Subj.
(c) Future Indicative   becomes Future Subj. or Conditional

Examples:

(a) „Ich **schreibe.**"   Er sagt (sagte), er **schreibe** *or* **schriebe.**
(b) „Ich **schrieb.**"
„Ich **habe geschrieben.**"   Er sagt (sagte), er **habe** *or* **hätte geschrieben.**
„Ich **hatte geschrieben.**"
(c) „Ich **werde schreiben.**"   Er sagt (sagte), er **werde** *or* **würde schreiben.**

3. The subjunctive forms of the present, present perfect, and future are used primarily in formal style; the subjunctive forms of the past, past perfect, and conditional are preferred in conversation and informal writing. But if the subjunctive forms of the present, present perfect,

or future are indistinguishable from the corresponding indicative forms, the subjunctive of the past, past perfect, or conditional is used:

Er sagte, sie **gingen** (*not* gehen), sie **hätten** (*not* haben), sie **würden** (*not* werden)

d. Indirect Questions

Questions in indirect discourse are expressed like indirect statements. Indirect questions are introduced by **ob** or interrogatives, such as **wer, wie, wo, wann**:

Er fragte ihn, **ob er Zeit habe (hätte).**   *if he had time.*
           wer mir helfen könne (könnte).   *who could help me.*
           wann sie angekommen sei (wäre).   *when she had arrived.*
           wo er ihn treffen werde (würde).   *where he would meet him.*

When the main verb is in the present tense, the indirect question remains in the indicative:

„Wie alt bist du?"   Er **fragt** dich, wie alt du **bist.**
„Wohin gehen Sie?"   Er **fragt** Sie, wohin Sie **gehen.**

e. Indirect Imperatives

An indirect command becomes a form of the auxiliary **sollen** with infinitive (English *should*):

Sie sagte, ich **solle (sollte) kommen.**

When the main verb is in the present tense, the indirect imperative remains in the indicative:

Deine Mutter **sagt,** du **sollst** nach Hause **kommen.**

f. Subjunctive Formulas: *could have; should have*

Sie **hätten** ihm **helfen können.**
You could have helped him.
Sie **hätten** ihm **helfen sollen.**
You should have helped him.

g. "As if" Construction

Er tut, **als ob er viel Einfluß hätte.**
He acts as if he had much influence.
Er tut, **als ob er viel Einfluß gehabt hätte.**
He acts as if he had had much influence.

Note: **Ob** may be omitted; as a result, inverted word order is used:

Er tut, **als hätte er viel Einfluß.**

Exercises

E.53 *Translate:*

1. Ich fragte ihn, ob seine Freunde mitkommen würden. 2. Wenn das Buch hier wäre, würde ich es lesen. 3. Er sagte mir, daß ich kommen solle. 4. Er sprach, als ob er Amerika entdeckt hätte. 5. Wäre er nur hier! 6. Alle sagten, daß es nicht möglich sei. 7. Sie glaubte, wir hätten ihn gesehen. 8. Hätte ich das gewußt, so hätte ich ihm das Geld nicht gegeben. 9. Das wäre möglich. 10. Wäre ich nur nicht so krank! 11. Wenn ich Zeit gehabt hätte, hätte ich ihm geholfen. 12. Sie sah aus, als sei sie krank. 13. Ich möchte noch eine Tasse Kaffee. 14. Das hätten Sie wissen sollen. 15. Dürfte ich Sie um Feuer bitten? 16. Er hätte es tun können. 17. Sie hätte es tun sollen. 18. Er möchte Ihnen etwas vorspielen. 19. Er würde gewiß besser spielen, wenn er mehr übte. 20. Er glaubte, es sei besser, nichts von seiner Krankheit zu erwähnen. 21. Seine Freunde hätten es ihm nicht geglaubt. 22. Sie sollten ihn wenigstens dem Namen nach kennen. 23. Sein Leben wäre einfacher gewesen, wenn er die Verantwortung nicht auf sich genommen hätte. 24. Könnten Sie es mir erklären? 25. Wenn die Ursache der Krankheit bekannt wäre, könnte man ihm helfen. 26. Wenn er sich nur über die Folgen klar gewesen wäre! 27. Wir hätten das Stück doch nicht spielen können. 28. Man glaubt, daß sie schon als Kind taub gewesen sei. 29. Wenn man es nur früher bemerkt hätte! 30. Man hätte ihr vielleicht helfen können.

E.54 *Using the correct forms of the subjunctive of* **sollen** *and* **können,** *change the following sentences to read:*

a. . . . should have
b. . . . could have

1. Er geht aufs Land. 2. Ich lese das Buch. 3. Sie stehen früher auf. 4. Er besucht seinen alten Freund. 5. Sie gibt dem Mann etwas Geld. 6. Ich arbeite mehr.

E.55 *Using the "should have" construction, precede each of the sentences in E.54 with* **Ich weiß, daß** . . . (*for example,* I know that he should have gone to the country).

E.56 *Express in German:*

1. If I told you that, you would not understand it. 2. They asked her when she would visit them. 3. If the book were interesting, he would read it. 4. Had I only known that! 5. They looked as if they were tired. 6. Had he had the money, he would have bought the big house. 7. You should have learned more. 8. He ate as if he were hungry. 9. She would be happy if he were here. 10. I could have danced all night.

E.57 *Change the following to indirect discourse:*

1. Barbara erzählte uns: „Ich wohnte zuerst bei der Familie Müller.“ 2. Sie sagt uns: „Die Müllers behandeln mich wie ihre Tochter.“ 3. Sie berichtet weiter: „Mein Zimmer war nie warm genug.“ 4. Frau Müller kritisierte: „Sie haben das elektrische Licht gestern bis zwei Uhr brennen lassen.“ 5. Sie antwortete der Frau: „Ich habe aber studiert.“ 6. Deutsche Kommilitonen sagten mir: „Du hast recht.“ 7. Meine Freundin fragte mich: „Was ist eine richtige Wirtin?“ 8. Sie erzählte mir: „So etwas ist mir auch passiert.“ 9. Er fragt: „Muß das erwähnt werden?“ 10. Der Lehrer sagte zu dem Schüler: „Lesen Sie, bitte!“ 11. Die junge Studentin fragte: „Ist jedes Land durch seine Vergangenheit beeinflußt?“ 12. Mein Freund dachte: „Der Mann hatte sich schon vorgestellt.“ 13. Verwundert fragte ich den Studenten: „Woher wissen Sie das?“ 14. Frau Müller warnte die amerikanische Studentin: „Gebrauchen Sie nicht zu viel warmes Wasser für Ihr Bad!“ 15. Die amerikanischen Studentinnen haben erklärt: „Wir können das nicht glauben.“ 16. Der Professor sagte: „Ich konnte ihr nicht helfen.“ 17. Larry fragte seinen Freund: „Wirst du länger in Wien bleiben?“ 18. Er behauptete: „Meine Freundin hat sich immer für Musik interessiert.“ 19. Ich dachte: „Das Konzert beginnt um 8 Uhr.“ 20. Mir wurde gesagt: „Es hat bereits um 7 begonnen.“

50. Present Participle

The present participle is formed by adding **-d** to the infinitive: spiele**nd,** lächel**nd.** It is used as an adjective or as an adverb:

das **lächelnde** Kind . . .
the smiling child
das Kind sagte **lächelnd** . . .
the child said (smilingly) with a smile . . .
Er spricht **überraschend** gut Deutsch.
He speaks German surprisingly well.

51. Past Participle

Apart from its use with auxiliaries to form the present perfect, past perfect, and the passive voice, the past participle is used as:

a. Adjective:

> ein viel **gelesener** Roman
> *a much-read novel*

b. Predicate Adjective:

> Das Büro ist **geschlossen.**
> *The office is closed.*

c. Predicate after **kommen:**

> Er kam **gelaufen.**
> *He came running.*

52. Word Order in Main Clauses

a. Normal Word Order

Normal word order is used in main clauses, that is, in direct statements. The subject stands first and is immediately followed by the finite verb, the inflected part of the verb, which has the personal endings. The uninflected part of the verb (infinitive or past participle) stands last:

> **Er kommt** morgen in Bonn **an.**
> **Er ist** gestern in Bonn **angekommen.**
> **Er wird** morgen in Bonn **ankommen.**
> **Er soll** morgen in Bonn **ankommen.**

Note 1: No part of the sentence can stand between the subject and the verb:

> **Ich rauche nie.**   *I never smoke.*
> **Er wurde bald berühmt.** *He soon became famous.*

Note 2: The subject may be modified by attributes or clauses:

> **Der junge amerikanische Student** kommt morgen in Bonn an.
> **Der junge Student, den ich in New York kennengelernt habe,** kommt morgen in **Bonn an.**

b. Inverted Word Order

For stylistic variety or to emphasize a particular element, a main clause may be started with an element other than the subject, even with a dependent clause. The finite verb must remain in second position, followed by the subject. This reversal of normal word order is called inverted word order:

Morgen **wird er** nach Köln **fahren.**
Nach Köln **wird er** nicht **fahren.**
Seinen Bruder **hat er** auf dieser Reise nicht **besucht.**
Als er in Köln war, **hat er** seinen Bruder **besucht.**

Note 1: Only one element of the main clause may precede the verb:

> **Auf meiner Reise nach Deutschland** habe ich voriges Jahr meinen Bruder besucht.
> *On my trip to Germany last year I visited my brother.*

Note 2: The first element, as long as it remains a single entity, may be modified:

> **Voriges Jahr, als ich meinen Bruder besuchte,** wurde ich krank.

Note 3: Words and phrases such as **ja, nein, im Gegenteil** (*on the contrary*), which are separated by a comma, do not affect word order:

> Nein, **er war** nicht in Köln.
> Im Gegenteil, **ich habe** nichts bezahlt.

Note 4: The coordinating conjunctions **aber** and **und** do not affect word order.

> **Aber ich werde** zu Hause **bleiben,** denn es regnet.

Note 5: The most common coordinating conjunctions are:

aber	*but*
denn	*for*
oder	*or*
sondern	*but*
und	*and*
entweder . . . oder	*either . . . or*
weder . . . noch	*neither . . . nor*

Inverted word order is also used:

1. In questions:

> **Kommt er** morgen an?
> Wann **ist er angekommen?**

Note: Questions with **Wer** have normal word order: **Wer ist** gestern **angekommen?**

2. In imperatives:

Gehen Sie!

3. In wishes:

Wäre ich nur zu Hause **geblieben!**
If only I had stayed at home.

53. Word Order in Dependent Clauses

a. A dependent clause has a relationship of dependence to the main clause. In a dependent clause introduced by a subordinating conjunction, **an** interrogative or a relative pronoun, the finite verb stands last. The infinitive or past participle immediately precedes the finite verb. If the double-infinitive construction occurs, the finite verb immediately precedes the double infinitive:

Er hat seinen Freund nicht besucht, weil er keine Zeit **hatte.**
                                                    weil er arbeiten **mußte.**
                                                    weil er **hat** arbeiten müssen.

Wissen Sie, wer ihm geholfen **hat?**
Köln, das mir sehr gefallen **hat,** werde ich wieder besuchen.

Note 1: When **daß** is omitted in indirect discourse, the finite verb is second in the subordinate clause:

Sie sagte, sie **sei** krank.
(Instead of) Sie sagte, daß sie krank **sei.**

Note 2: When **wenn** is omitted in conditional clauses, the finite verb is first:

Regnet es, so gehen wir ins Kino.
(Instead of) Wenn es **regnet,** gehen wir ins Kino.

Note 3: When **ob** or **wenn** is omitted in **als ob** or **als wenn** clauses, the finite verb follows **als:**

Er tat, **als hätte** er mich nicht verstanden.
(Instead of) Er tat, **als ob** er mich nicht verstanden **hätte.**

b. Subordinating Conjunctions

als	*when*	**ob**	*if, whether*
bevor	*before*	**obgleich, obwohl**	*although*
bis	*until*	**sobald**	*as soon as*
da	*as, since*	**trotzdem**	*although*
damit	*so that*	**während**	*while*
ehe	*before*	**weil**	*because*
falls	*in case*	**wenn**	*if, when, whenever*
nachdem	*after*		

54. Word Order within a Clause

a. Noun Objects

An indirect noun object (dative) precedes a direct noun object (accusative):

Er gibt **seinem Freund den Brief.**

b. Pronoun Objects

A direct pronoun object normally precedes an indirect pronoun object:

Er gibt **ihn ihm.**

A pronoun object precedes a noun object:

Er gibt **ihm den Brief.**
Er gibt **ihn seinem Freund.**

In inverted and dependent word order, an object pronoun usually precedes a subject noun:

Dann gab **ihm mein Bruder** den Brief.
Als **ihm mein Bruder** den Brief gab, . . .

c. Reflexive Pronouns

In a main clause, the reflexive pronoun follows the finite verb, except when the subject is a pronoun and inverted word order is used:

Hans **wäscht sich** die Hände.
Jetzt **wäscht sich Hans** die Hände.
But:
Jetzt **wäscht er sich** die Hände.

In a dependent clause, the reflexive pronoun precedes the subject, except when the subject is a pronoun:

Wenn **sich Hans** die Hände **wäscht,** ...
But:
Wenn **er sich** die Hände **wäscht,** ...

d. Expressions of Time

1. Expressions of time precede noun objects:

   Ich habe **jetzt** keine Zeit.

2. Expressions of time precede expressions of place:

   Wir fahren **heute in die Stadt.**

e. Adverbs

The order of adverbs and adverbial phrases is usually as follows: (1) cause, (2) time, (3) manner, (4) place, (5) degree:

Ich habe **trotz der Hitze** (1) **gestern abend** (2) **wider Erwarten** (3) **in meinem Zimmer** (4) **gut** (5) studieren **können**.

f. Position of **nicht** and **nie**

1. In simple tenses, **nicht** and **nie** stand at the end of the clause, but in a dependent clause they precede the finite verb:

   Er versteht mich **nicht / nie.**
   Da er mich **nicht / nie** versteht, ...

   In compound tenses **nicht** and **nie** precede the infinitive or participle:

   Ich werde den Roman **nicht / nie** lesen.
   Da ich den Roman **nicht / nie** gelesen habe, ...

2. **Nicht** and **nie** precede a separable prefix, a predicate adjective, a predicate noun, an adverb, or a prepositional phrase:

   Sie kommt **nicht / nie** mit.
   Da er **nicht / nie** müde wird, ...
   Er ist **nicht** sein Doktor.
   Da er **nicht / nie** laut genug spricht, ...
   Sein Wagen ist **nicht / nie** in der Garage.

3. When negating a particular word, **nicht** and **nie** immediately precede that word:

   Er hat **nicht / nie** seine Mutter, sondern seine Freundin angerufen.

Exercises

E.58 *Translate:*

1. He is reading; he is reading the book; he is not reading the book.
2. You are a student; you are not a student; he is not German. 3. He opens the book; he doesn't open the book. 4. Larry saw the play in Munich during his summer semester. 5. It is warm today; today it is warm; it is not warm today. 6. I know this gentleman; this gentleman I know; I do not know this gentleman. 7. We are going to Europe this summer; this summer we are going to Europe. 8. Don't come into my cabin, or I'll tell the captain. 9. I don't have a sister but a brother.
10. Let's wait here, for it will rain soon. 11. He left the house, but he went to visit his friends. 12. Show me the picture; show it to me; don't show it to me. 13. Give the professor this book; give him this book; give it to him. 14. I have told him nothing; I will tell him nothing.
15. By whom is the book being illustrated? By whom was the book illustrated? 16. I get up every morning at seven o'clock. 17. She had brought him along; she is bringing him along. 18. It was impossible for me to get up so early. 19. He did not look at me; he is not looking at me; he had looked at me. 20. I know that he got up early; I know that he will get up early. 21. Tell me when he comes home. 22. Let's help him, even though he doesn't deserve it. 23. He couldn't answer because he hadn't read the book. 24. Do it while you have the time. 25. If the poems interest you, you will read more of them. 26. How old is he? Do you know how old he is? He knows how old he is. 27. Ask him where there is a good restaurant. 28. I would like to speak with the student who was absent yesterday. 29. He is the man whose wife won the 100 dollars.
30. These are the writers who visited several universities in Europe.
31. These are men whom one cannot help. 32. He said that he had seen him fall. 33. He was so sick that we were allowed to visit him only once.
34. He says that it will get cold. 35. His mistake was discovered by the director on Wednesday. 36. Yesterday when he came home, it was very warm. 37. You look as if you had not slept. 38. Whenever I work, I get tired. 39. He worked until it became dark. 40. I am telling you so that you know. 41. He woke up because she made too much noise. 42. He will visit Italy before he leaves Europe. 43. After he had arrived in Germany, he visited friends in Hamburg. 44. He asked me whether I had understood the official. 45. Although he is rich, he is not happy. 46. As soon as she arrived, she called up her mother. 47. I was not able to read while I was ill. 48. As she said that, she sat down. 49. If I had time, I would visit him. 50. Even though he has attended a university, he does not know much.

55. Cardinal Numbers

0	null	14	vierzehn	60	sechzig
1	eins	15	fünfzehn	70	siebzig
2	zwei	16	sechzehn	80	achtzig
3	drei	17	siebzehn	90	neunzig
4	vier	18	achtzehn	100	(ein)hundert
5	fünf	19	neunzehn	101	hundert(und)eins
6	sechs	20	zwanzig	115	hundertfünfzehn
7	sieben	21	einundzwanzig	188	hundertachtundachtzig
8	acht	22	zweiundzwanzig	200	zweihundert
9	neun	23	dreiundzwanzig	1000	(ein)tausend
10	zehn	30	dreißig	10,000	zehntausend
11	elf	31	einunddreißig	100,000	hunderttausend
12	zwölf	40	vierzig	1,000,000	eine Million
13	dreizehn	50	fünfzig	1,000,000,000	eine Milliarde

Note spelling and usage:

a. **sechzehn, siebzehn; sechzig, siebzig**

b. **1938 Stück: eintausendneunhundertachtunddreißig Stück**
1938 pieces

As a year: **neunzehnhundertachtunddreißig**

c. The word **hundert** may not be omitted, as in English.

d. The numeral **eins** becomes **ein** before a noun and is inflected like the indefinite article: **ein** Buch, **eines** Buches, etc. The other cardinal numbers are not inflected. An adjective following such a number takes the endings -e, -er, -en, -e:

Er hat **zwei (vier) neue** Bücher. *He has two (four) new books.*

56. Ordinal Numbers

Ordinal numbers are adjectives formed from the cardinals by adding -t to the numbers 2 to 19 and -st to 20 and up. The examples below are given in the masculine nominative singular. Ordinal numbers take the same endings as a preceded adjective:

1st	**der erste**	19th	**der neunzehnte**
2nd	**der zweite**	20th	**der zwanzigste**
3rd	**der dritte**	21st	**der einundzwanzigste**
4th	**der vierte**	56th	**der sechsundfünfzigste**
5th	**der fünfte**	100th	**der hundertste**
6th	**der sechste**		

Er kauft **sein drittes** Buch.   *He buys his third book.*
Er hat **am elften** Mai geschrieben.   *He wrote on the 11th of May.*

57. Expressing Dates and Age

Der wievielte ist heute?   *What is today's date?*
Heute ist der fünfte November. (or)
Heute haben wir den fünften November.
Wann haben Sie Geburtstag?   *When is your birthday?*
Am einundzwanzigsten August.
Wann sind Sie geboren?   *When were you born?*
Ich bin (im Jahre) 1948 geboren.   *I was born in 1948.*
Wann wurde Schiller geboren?   *When was Schiller born?*
Er wurde (im Jahre) 1759 geboren.   *He was born in 1759.*

58. Names of Days

(der) **Sonntag**	**Donnerstag**
Montag	**Freitag**
Dienstag	**Sonnabend (Samstag)**
Mittwoch	

59. Names of Months

(der) **Januar**	**Juli**
Februar	**August**
März	**September**
April	**Oktober**
Mai	**November**
Juni	**Dezember**

60. Telling Time

Wie spät ist es? (or) **Wieviel Uhr ist es?** *What time is it?*

1:00 **Es ist eins** (or) **Es ist ein Uhr.**
9:00 **Es ist neun (Uhr).**

9:15 **Es ist Viertel nach neun** (or) **Es ist (ein) Viertel zehn.** (that is, a quarter of
the tenth hour has passed)
9:30 **Es ist halb zehn.** (that is, half of the tenth hour has passed)
9:45 **Es ist Viertel vor zehn.** (or) **Es ist dreiviertel zehn.**
9:05 **Es ist fünf (Minuten) nach neun.**
9:25 **Es ist fünf (Minuten) vor halb zehn.**
9:35 **Es ist fünf (Minuten) nach halb zehn.**
9:50 **Es ist zehn (Minuten) vor zehn.**

61. Expressions of Time

a. Um wieviel Uhr?   *At what time?*
Um 6 (Uhr).   *At 6 o'clock.*
Gegen 6 (Uhr).   *About* (shortly before) *6 o'clock.*
Er kam Punkt 6 (Uhr) an.   *He arrived at 6 o'clock sharp.*

b. heute abend   *tonight* (before bedtime)
heute nacht   *tonight* (after bedtime); *last night* (during the night)
heute früh   *this morning*
morgen früh   *tomorrow morning*
gestern abend   *last night*
vorgestern   *day before yesterday*
übermorgen   *day after tomorrow*

c. The genitive is used to denote indefinite time:

eines Tages   *one day*

d. The accusative is used to express duration and definite time:

jeden Tag	*every day*	**den ganzen Tag**	*all day*
jede Woche	*every week*	**die ganze Woche**	*all week*
jedes Jahr	*every year*	**das ganze Jahr**	*the whole year*
nächsten Montag	*next Monday*	**acht Tage**	*a week*
nächste Woche	*next week*	**vierzehn Tage**	*two weeks*
nächstes Jahr	*next year*		
voriges Jahr	*last year*		

e. Prepositions that take either the dative or accusative are used with the
dative in expressions of time:

am Sonntag	*on Sunday*	**in zwei Tagen**	*in two days*
am Morgen	*in the morning*	**vor drei Jahren**	*three years ago*
im Frühling	*in spring*		

Part Two

Aids
for
Reading

A. False Cognates

aktuell	*current; topical*
also	*therefore, then*
die Art	*kind, manner*
bald	*soon*
das Beet	*flower bed*
bekommen	*to get, receive*
das Boot	*boat*
brav	*honest, good, well-behaved*
denn	*for, because*
eben	*level; just*
eventuell	*possibly, perhaps*
fast	*almost*
genial	*ingenious*
das Gift	*poison*
der Gürtel	*belt*
halten	*to hold; to stop*
die Hochschule	*university*
das Klosett	*toilet*
die Kost	*food; board*
die Lektüre	*reading*
das Maß	*measure*
die Novelle	*short story*
passen	*to fit well*
der Platz	*seat; room; place*
prüfen	*to test*
restlos	*completely*
der Rat	*advice*
der Rock	*skirt*
schmal	*narrow*
der Sinn	*sense, meaning*
sinnvoll	*significant, meaningful*
spenden	*to donate*
der Teller	*plate*
überall	*everywhere*
das Volk	*people, nation*
vor	*in front of; ago*
weil	*because*
wer	*who*
wirken	*to take effect*

Translate:

1. Die Flüchtlinge bekommen wärmere Kleider, wenn es kalt wird. 2. Ich bin eben angekommen und habe noch kein Hotel. 3. In Amerika tragen die meisten Männer Gürtel und keine Hosenträger. 4. Nach der Lektüre verstand ich den Vortrag über diese Novelle viel besser. 5. Wert und Maß sind Worte, die die große Masse nicht leicht versteht. 6. Weißt du, wer es ist? 7. Reich mir noch einmal das Bandmaß, der Anzug für den Herrn Doktor muß passen. 8. Kann ein sündiges Leben ein sinnvolles Leben sein? 9. Überall war der Gesamteindruck derselbe: Hübsche Mädchen in häßlichen Overalls. 10. Das Aspirin wirkt; jetzt kann ich wieder arbeiten. 11. Seine Hände sind klein und sehr schmal. 12. Kein Wunder, daß du restlos erschöpft bist bei deiner rastlosen Arbeit im Büro. 13. Wenn du hier ruhig spielst und brav bist, bekommst du dann zwei Stück Schokolade, Karlchen. 14. Er ist fast so schnell gelaufen wie der finnische Läufer. 15. Weißt du, was in dem Geschenkpaket war? Gift in Bonbons. 16. Schreiben Sie an Professor Buswick, er kennt die deutschen Hochschulen und höheren Schulen. 17. Diese Lektüre ist sehr sinnvoll. Man spricht überall davon. 18. Er ist genial, sein Bruder ist nur intelligent. 19. Wir haben eventuell noch ein Zimmer für Sie, aber am Ende sollten Sie sich doch ein anderes Hotel suchen. 20. Hier halten wir. Würden Sie einen Augenblick meinen Hund halten, der darf nicht mit ins Hotel. 21. Nehmen wir an, diese Metallkugel rollt auf einer ebenen Fläche. 22. Sie müssen noch Lateinisch lernen, denn dann erst verstehen Sie Vergil, Horaz und viele andere große Schriftsteller dieser Zeit. 23. Bald werde ich kahl sein. 24. Er sprach in seiner letzten Rede nur über aktuelle Probleme. 25. Diese Art von Diplomatie ist eine Kunst. 26. Die Kosten für Zimmer und Kost sind nicht hoch. 27. Er trat mit seinen schweren Seemannsstiefeln ins Boot. 28. Von meinem Bett aus sehe ich den Garten mit den schönen Beeten. 29. Es regnet. Auch heute wird also nichts aus unserem Picknick. 30. Vor einer Stunde wartete er noch vor der Bibliothek. 31. Wir dürfen das Geld jetzt nicht ausgeben, er hat es uns fürs nächste Picknick gespendet. 32. Ich warne euch; wir werden über Felsen klettern. Jetzt hat sie sich Rock und Bluse ruiniert. 33. Hier ist mein Rat: Tu was gegen die Ratten in deinem Haus! 34. Das Buch liegt auf meinem Platz im Bus, verlier aber meine Stelle nicht! 35. Ich ärgere mich über ihn, weil er im Kino war, während wir trainierten. 36. Bei einigen Völkern war es Sitte, die alten Verwandten zu töten. 37. Der Kassierer sah auf seinen Teller, aber er aß nicht. 38. Der Sinn der Sünde ist heute anders als im Mittelalter. 39. Prüft alles und behaltet das Beste! 40. Das Klosett ist links von diesem Wandschrank.

B. Troublesome Idioms and Constructions

1. als

a. after comparative: *than*

Er ist **älter als** ich.
He is older than I.

b. before noun: *as*

Ich kenne ihn nur **als meinen Arzt.**
I know him only as my physician.

c. verb at end of sentence: *when*

Als er in Amerika **war,** . . .
When he was in America, . . .

d. followed by verb in subjunctive: *as if*

Er tut, **als wüßte er** das nicht.
He acts as if he did not know that.

e. nichts als: *nothing but*

Ich kann **nichts** anderes tun **als** nachgeben.
I can't do anything else but give in.

2. auch

a. *also, too*

Wir fliegen **auch** nach Frankfurt.
We are also flying to Frankfurt.

b. initial position, followed by subject: *also, too*

Auch er weiß das.
He too knows that.

c. in combination with **nicht** or **kein:** *either*

Ich gehe **auch nicht.**
I am not going either.
Er hat **auch kein** Geld.
He doesn't have any money either.

3. da

a. *there*

> **Da** ist er.
> *There he is.*

b. *then*

> **Da** stand er plötzlich auf.
> *Then he suddenly got up.*

c. verb at end of clause: *since*

> **Da er** nicht **kam,** sind wir gegangen.
> *Since he did not come, we left.*

4. da(r)-Compounds

a. *the fact* (*that*)

> Er ist stolz **darauf,** daß er gut Deutsch lesen kann.
> *He is proud of the fact that he can read German well.*
> Er machte mich **darauf** aufmerksam, daß es sehr spät war.
> *He called my attention to the fact that it was very late.*

b. Disregard **da(r)-** and translate the verb of the dependent clause or phrase with the *-ing* form:

> Er erreichte sein Ziel **dadurch, daß er** jeden Tag etwas **sparte.**
> *He reached his goal by saving something every day.*

> Er bestand **darauf,** der erste **zu sein.**
> *He insisted on being the first.*

c. Disregard the **da(r)**-compound:

> Ich zweifle **daran,** daß er Erfolg haben wird.
> *I doubt that he will be successful.*

Translate:

1. Da er noch im Bett liegt und schläft, gehen wir ohne ihn jagen.   2. Er ärgert sich darüber, daß ihr ihn nicht eingeladen habt.   3. Man hat nichts als Schwierigkeiten mit ihm.   4. Er verdiente sich etwas Geld dadurch, daß er Touristen die Stadt und ihre Sehenswürdigkeiten zeigte.   5. Ich habe nichts dagegen, daß er bleibt.   6. Ich habe oft daran gedacht, ihn um das nötige Geld zu bitten.   7. Er schrie, als wollten wir ihn ermorden.

8. „Auch du, Brutus" waren die letzten Worte Caesars. 9. Ich kenne ihn nur als einen Angestellten, der viel älter ist als ich. 10. Da liegt er und schläft noch. 11. „Als Deutschland noch jung war, da war ich auch jung", sagte Goethe einmal. 12. Er bestand darauf, die Rechnung zu bezahlen. 13. Ich wußte nichts davon, daß er krank gewesen war. 14. Ich warte darauf, daß die Medizin wirkt. 15. Ich kann ihm auch nicht helfen.

5. Demonstrative Use of der

a. *that one, those*

Geben Sie mir **den** / **die**.
Give me that one / those.

b. *the latter's*

Meine Mutter, meine Schwester und **deren** Freundin haben uns gestern besucht.
My mother, my sister and her (the latter's) girl friend visited us yesterday.

6. doch

a. used in place of **ja** to contradict a negative statement or to answer a negative question affirmatively when a negative answer is expected:

Das ist nicht wahr. —**Doch.**
That is not true. — Yes, it is.
Hat er die Rechnung nicht bezahlt? —**Doch.**
Hasn't he paid the bill? —Oh, yes, he has.

b. used to strengthen a statement—*after all, surely, anyway*

Er ist **doch** gekommen.
He did come after all.
Ich habe es ihm **doch** gesagt.
I did tell him anyway.

c. when used at the beginning of a sentence—*however:*

Doch niemand wollte ihm helfen.
No one wanted to help him, however.

d. when used in a question, the speaker asks for confirmation:

POSITIVE: Sie kennen ihn **doch?**
          You know him, don't you?
NEGATIVE: Sie haben ihn **doch** nicht kritisiert?
          I hope you didn't criticize him.

e. used with imperatives to urge action:

Sagen Sie es **doch!**
Why don't you say it? (or) *Well, say it.* (or) *Do say it.*

7. einmal

a. The shortened form **mal** is frequently used for emphasis, but it often has no English equivalent:

Denken Sie **mal!**
Just imagine.
Sagen Sie **mal!**
Tell me!

b. noch einmal (mal): *once more*

Sagen Sie es bitte **noch einmal!**
Please say it again (once more).

c. schon einmal (mal): *already*

Ich habe den Film **schon einmal** gesehen.
I have already seen the film (once).

d. in a question, **schon einmal** means *ever:*

Waren Sie **schon einmal** in Deutschland?
Have you ever been in Germany?

e. nicht einmal (mal): *not even*

Er hat mir **nicht einmal** eine Postkarte geschickt.
He didn't even send me a postcard.

f. auf einmal: *suddenly*

Auf einmal stand er auf.
Suddenly he got up.

8. -er Ending

a. adjective ending after **ein-**word

kein neu**er** Wagen
no new car

b. comparative and adjective ending

ein schön**erer** Wagen
a more beautiful car

c. comparative ending of adverb and adjective ending

ein schnell**er** wachsen**der** Baum
a faster growing tree

d. genitive plural adjective ending

das Resultat genau**er** Untersuchungen
the result of exact investigations

e. comparative and genitive plural adjective ending

das Resultat genau**erer** Untersuchungen
the result of more exact investigations

Translate:

1. Waren Sie schon einmal in Afrika? 2. Mein schöner neuer Koffer ist verschwunden. 3. Du hast die Rede nicht verstanden. —Doch, ich war nur ein bißchen müde. 4. Da geht XY, der bekannte Filmstar. Kennen Sie den? 5. Die Leute in seinem Büro sollten das tun. Von denen kann er das aber nicht erwarten. 6. Die Dame ist eine bekannte Journalistin. —So? Von der habe ich noch nie etwas gelesen. 7. Er hat nicht einmal „danke schön" gesagt. 8. Das sind die Spuren alter Formationen. Und hier haben wir Spuren noch älterer Formationen. 9. So ist unser Seeklima: erst herrlicher Sonnenschein, und dann auf einmal wird es kalt. 10. Hast du nie etwas von Goethe gelesen? —Doch, sehr viel. 11. Gehen Sie mal nach Hause und ruhen Sie sich aus! 12. Früher mußten Schüler der Höheren Schule die Mythen, die von Apollo, Hermes, Zeus und dessen Sohn Herkules handelten, genau kennen. 13. Spielen Sie die Stelle noch einmal und diesmal langsamer! 14. Ein älterer Herr ist nicht so alt wie ein alter Herr. 15. Er hat doch gesiegt; K.O. in der vierzehnten Runde.

9. erst

a. with expressions of time: *not only, only*

Wir sind **erst um acht Uhr** angekommen.
We didn't arrive until eight o'clock.
Er ist **erst zehn Jahre** alt.
He is only ten years old.

b. eben erst: *just (only) now*

Ich habe den Brief **eben erst** bekommen.
I got the letter just now.

c. erst recht: *all the more, nevertheless*

Der Vater hat ihm verboten zu rauchen, aber nun raucht er **erst recht.**
His father told him not to smoke, but now he smokes all the more.

10. es

a. impersonal: **es gibt** *there is, there are;* **es sind** *there are, they are*

Es hat immer Leute **gegeben,** die . . .
There have always been people who . . .
Es sind nur zehn Studenten anwesend.
There are only ten students present.
Wer sind diese jungen Leute? —**Es sind** Vertreter der Studentenschaft.
Who are these young people? —They are representatives of the student body.

b. introducing the real subject; **es** is not translated:

Es wird ein Versuch gemacht.
An experiment is being made.

11. ganz

a. used as adjective: *all (of), the whole*

Ich habe mein **ganzes** Geld ausgegeben.
I have spent all my money.
Die **ganze** Welt hat davon gehört.
The whole world has heard of it.

b. used as adverb: *quite, very*

Sie spielt **ganz gut** Klavier.
She plays the piano quite well.
Das Hotel ist **ganz nahe** beim Bahnhof.
The hotel is very close to the station.

12. gehen

a. may express mechanical motion: *to work, run, be*

Der Fahrstuhl **geht** nicht.
The elevator doesn't work.
Meine Uhr **geht** nicht.
My watch isn't running.
Seine Uhr **geht** nach.
His watch is slow.

b. Idioms

Geht das?
Will that do? (or) *Is that possible?*
Das geht nicht.
That won't do.

Translate:

1. Er will das nicht? Nun tue ich es erst recht. 2. Ruf die Garage an, der Starter geht nicht! 3. Ich bin noch ganz müde von der Wanderung. 4. Es gibt keine Bären in Afrika. 5. Du darfst das Paket erst Weihnachten aufmachen. 6. Es spricht jetzt der deutsche Bundeskanzler. 7. Ihre Uhr geht vor. 8. Es ist ein Löwe in der Nähe; hier sind die Spuren. 9. So geht das nicht. 10. Er spricht ganz wie sein Vater. 11. Ganz Amerika kennt den österreichischen Dichter Kafka. 12. Er hat die ganze Wurst aufgegessen. Er hat die Wurst ganz aufgegessen. 13. Das ist erst gestern geschehen. 14. Was für Tanks kommen da? —Es sind amerikanische Tanks. 15. Es wird niemand mitgehen. 16. Es wird in unserem Krankenhaus jeder Patient aufgenommen. 17. Wie du es machst, geht das nicht.

13. gelingen—gelangen

a. gelingen, gelang, ist gelungen: *to succeed, be successful*

Es **gelang ihm** endlich, den Brief zu entziffern.
He finally succeeded in deciphering the letter.

b. gelangen, gelangte, ist gelangt: *to arrive at, reach, attain*

Der Brief **gelangte** nicht in die richtigen Hände.
The letter didn't reach the right person.

14. gelten

a. gelten: *to be valid*

Die Mark **gilt** 25 Cents.
A mark is worth 25 cents.

b. gelten als: *to be considered*

Er **gilt als** Fachmann.
He is considered an expert.

c. gelten für or **von:** *to be true of, apply to*

Was **für** dich **gilt, gilt** auch **für** ihn.
What applies to you applies to him, too.
Das **gilt** auch **von** ihm.
That is true of him also.

d. es gilt . . . zu *is the thing to do; to be a question of*

Jetzt **gilt es,** nicht den Kopf **zu verlieren.**
The thing to do is to keep our heads.
Es galt, den Hügel **zu erobern.**
It was a question of conquering the hill.

15. halten

a. halten: *to keep*

Wie lange werden die Nationen **Frieden halten?**
How long will the nations keep peace?

b. halten für: *to consider, to take for*

Ich **halte** ihn **für** einen tüchtigen Lehrer.
I consider him a capable teacher.

c. halten von: *to think of*

Was **halten** Sie **von** seiner Arbeit?
What do you think of his work?

16. immer

a. intensifies the comparative and **wieder:**

Das Rad drehte sich **immer schneller.**
The wheel turned faster and faster.
Er sagte es **immer wieder.**
He said it again and again.

b. reinforces **noch: immer noch:** (emphatic) *still*

Er hat mir **immer noch** nicht geschrieben.
He still hasn't written me.

Translate:

1. Es gelang ihm mit Hilfe eines Küchenmessers, die hintere Tür zu öffnen.
2. So gelangte er auf den Hof, wo er sein Pferd fand und davongaloppierte. 3. Er wurde immer schwächer. 4. Er hält Hühner in seinem Garten. 5. Ein Dollar gilt 4 DM (Deutsche Mark). 6. Heine galt als der witzigste Schriftsteller seiner Zeit. 7. Er ist immer noch nicht zurück. 8. Was halten Sie davon? 9. Es galt, den Fehler in unserem Experiment zu entdecken. 10. Ich halte ihn für einen Holländer. 11. Gilt mein Paß noch? 12. Er gilt als der beste Mann in seinem Fach. 13. Er stellt immer wieder dieselbe Frage. 14. Er hält sein Wort nicht; wie kannst du da erwarten, daß er dies Versprechen hält? 15. Ein Prophet gilt nichts in seinem Vaterlande.

17. indem

a. indicates that an act takes place simultaneously with another one: *while, as*

Indem er sich tief **verbeugte, fiel ihm das Geld** aus der Tasche.
While he was bowing low, the money fell from his pocket.
„Gut", sagte er, **indem** er aufstand.
"Good," he said, as he got up.

b. indicates reason or cause: *by* plus *-ing* form

Er zeigte sich als wahrer Freund, **indem** er ihm half.
He showed himself a true friend by helping him.
Er verdiente sich etwas Geld, **indem** er Privatstunden gab.
He earned some money by giving private lessons.

18. Intensifiers of Prepositions (often without equivalent words in English)

Oben auf dem Dach ist ein Storchnest.
On top of the roof is a stork's nest.
von Anfang **an**
from the beginning
von meinem Fenster **aus**
from my window
vom Gebirge **her**
from the mountains
nach der Stadt **zu**
in the direction of the town

19. ja

a. unstressed; to give a statement a more positive emphasis:

Hier sind Sie **ja.**
Why, here you are.
Ich habe es dir **ja** gesagt.
I told you so, didn't I?
Ich arbeite **ja.**
I am working. (stress the auxiliary)

b. stressed; to add force to a command:

Schreiben Sie **ja!**
Be sure to write.
Tu das **ja** nicht wieder!
Don't you do that again.

20. lang, as Adverb of Time

drei Jahre lang
for three years
jahrelang
for years

Translate:

1. Indem wir vor dem Hause saßen und sprachen, wurde es Nacht. 2. Die Tanks fuhren bis an die Brücke heran. 3. Das ist ja Herr Weiß! 4. Der Verwundete rettete sich das Leben, indem er so still lag, als ob er tot wäre. 5. Tu das ja, sonst wird er böse! 6. Drei Tage lang soll der Kaiser in Canossa vor dem Fenster des Papstes gestanden haben. 7. Vom Turm aus konnten wir den Rhein sehen. 8. „Gut", sagte er, indem er aufstand. 9. Er zeigte sich als wahrer Freund, indem er ihm noch einmal half. 10. Sagen Sie das ja nicht dem Direktor!

21. sich lassen

a. If the subject is a thing or an abstraction, **läßt sich** means *can be* and **ließ sich,** *could be.* The German infinitive is equivalent to an English past participle:

Dieser Wagen **läßt sich** nicht mehr **reparieren.**
This car cannot be repaired anymore.

Keine Lösung **ließ sich finden.**
No solution could be found.

b. If the subject is a person, **läßt sich** means *has* and **ließ sich,** *had.* The German infinitive is equivalent to an English past participle:

Lassen Sie **sich** die Haare **schneiden!**
Have your hair cut.
Er **ließ sich** eine neue Garage **bauen.**
He had a new garage built.

22. noch

a. implies continuation of an action or state: *still, yet*

Er wohnt **noch** in Berlin.
He is still living in Berlin.
Du wirst es **noch** bereuen.
You will regret it yet.

b. with expressions of time: *only, just, but . . . ago*

Noch letzte Woche habe ich ihn dort gesehen.
Only (Just) last week I saw him there.
I saw him there but a week ago.

c. noch ein: *another*

Geben Sie mir **noch ein** Glas Wasser!
Give me another glass of water.

d. noch einmal: *once more*

Sagen Sie es bitte **noch einmal!**
Please say it once more.

e. noch nicht: *not yet*

Er wußte es **noch nicht.**
He did not know it yet.

f. noch nichts: *not anything (as) yet*

Er hat mir **noch nichts** davon gesagt.
He has not told me anything about it yet.

g. noch nie: *never (yet)*

Er ist **noch nie** hier gewesen.
He has never (yet) been here.

23. nur

a. *only, merely*

> Er hat **nur einen Bruder.**
> *He has only one brother.*

b. adding reassurance to an imperative or a wish:

> **Kommen Sie nur** zu mir! Ich helfe Ihnen.
> *Just come to me. I'll help you.*
> **Wenn er nur** bald **käme!**
> *If he would only come soon.*

c. In a question, **nur** implies surprise:

> **Was wird sie nur denken?**
> *I wonder what she will think.*
> **Wie können Sie nur so etwas sagen?**
> *How can you say something like that?*

24. Reflexive Verbs

a. equivalent to English reflexive:

> **Er hat sich geschnitten.**
> *He cut himself.*

b. reflexive not expressed in English:

> **Sie hat sich** schnell **erholt.**
> *She recovered quickly.*

c. equivalent to English passive:

> Die Liebe zum Walde **zeigt sich** in vielen deutschen Märchen.
> *Love for the forest is shown in many German fairy tales.*

Translate:

1. Das läßt sich nicht ändern. Das ließ sich nicht ändern. 2. Haben Sie noch nichts von ihm gehört? 3. Kauf es doch, es kostet ja nur 3 DM! 4. Hast du dich entschuldigt? 5. Haben Sie es noch nicht verstanden? 6. So ein Experiment ließ sich damals nicht machen. 7. Er wollte sich nicht operieren lassen. 8. So etwas sagt sich leicht. 9. Sag mir nur nicht, du hättest das nicht gewußt! 10. Wo bist du denn nur gewesen? 11. Noch vor einer Woche kannte ich nicht einmal seinen Namen. 12. Bilden Sie

mir bitte noch einen Satz mit *noch!* 13. Lesen Sie den Satz noch einmal vor! 14. Bist du noch nie geflogen? 15. Ich habe noch nichts davon gehört.

25. schon

a. basic meaning: *already*

Schon im Jahre 1930 . . .
Already in the year 1930 . . .

b. with the present tense and expressions of time (equivalent to English present perfect progressive and expressions of time):

Wir **wohnen schon seit zwei Jahren** in dieser Wohnung.
We have been living in this apartment for two years.

c. to imply assurance or emphasis: *no doubt, surely, as a matter of fact*

Er wird dich **schon** erkennen.
He will surely recognize you.
Das ist **schon** wahr, aber weiß er es schon?
As a matter of fact, that is true, but does he know it already?

d. schon einmal

STATEMENT: Ich bin **schon einmal** dort gewesen.
         I have been there once.
QUESTION: Sind Sie **schon einmal** dort gewesen?
         Have you ever been there?

26. selbst

a. **Er selbst** hat es mir gesagt.
He himself told it to me.

b. **Selbst er** weiß es nicht.
Even he doesn't know it.

27. sollte

Does not automatically mean *should;* consider the following meanings in order: *ought to, was (supposed) to, should:*

Er **sollte** das wissen.
He ought to know this.

Er **sollte** um zehn Uhr hier sein.
He was supposed to be here at ten o'clock.
Er **sollte** das nicht tun.
He should not do this.

28. Special Uses of the Present Subjunctive

a. Some present subjunctive forms are found chiefly in formal German. They are expressed in English by *let*, *may*, or *should*, depending on the context:

let

Gehen wir!
Let's go.
Essen wir!
Let's eat.
A-C **sei** die Seite eines Dreiecks.
Let A-C be the side of a triangle.
Edel **sei** der Mensch, hilfreich und gut! (Goethe)
Let man be noble, helpful, and good!

may

Dieser Fall **diene** als Beispiel.
This case may serve as an example.
Er **ruhe** in Frieden!
May he rest in peace.

should

Man **erwarte** nicht zuviel von ihm.
One should not expect too much of him.
Der Leser **vergesse** nicht, daß sie damals sehr jung war.
The reader should not forget that she was very young at that time.

b. Directions on everyday objects in cookbooks or technical books often use a present subjunctive, where English uses an imperative:

Man schüttle die Flasche vor Gebrauch.
Shake the bottle before using.

Translate:

1. Du wirst schon einen Brief von ihr bekommen. 2. Gretchen und Lieschen haben diesen Kuchen selbst gebacken. 3. Sie sollten nicht so viel rauchen, das viele Rauchen soll sehr ungesund sein. 4. Selbst Gretchen

und Lieschen mochten den Kuchen nicht. 5. Alles sollte sich ändern, aber es hat sich nichts geändert. 6. Wie lange haben Sie diese Schmerzen schon? 7. Nehmen wir an, es war alles so, wie er sagt. 8. Man nehme nun aber nicht an, daß alles so war, wie er sagt. 9. Er ruhe in Frieden. 10. Man nehme ein Viertelliter Sahne, schlage sie gut und lange und mische dann drei Teelöffel Schokoladenpulver darunter. 11. Der Leser glaube nun nicht, daß all das in kurzer Zeit geschah. 12. Die Strecke A-B sei fünfzig m (Meter) lang. 13. „Er komme in unser Land", sagte der König, „und sehe mit eigenen Augen die Stärke unseres Heeres." 14. Ehe man diese Salbe gebraucht, gebe man dem Patienten ein Antibiotikum. 15. Dies Experiment mache man aber mit äußerster Vorsicht, damit sich keine Flamme bilde.

29. trotzdem

a. adverb: *nevertheless, just the same*

Trotzdem ist er sehr arm.
Nevertheless he is very poor.

b. conjunction (verb at end of sentence): *although*

Trotzdem er sehr arm **ist, . . .**
Although he is very poor, . . .

30. Verb First

a. command

Gehen Sie!
Go!

b. question

Haben Sie es gefunden?
Did you find it?

c. condition

Versucht man ihn zu überzeugen, dann . . .
If one tries to convince him, then . . .
Hatte er auch kein Geld, so . . .
Even though he had no money, . . .

d. wish

Wäre sie nur gekommen!
If she had only come!

31. während

a. preposition: *during*

Während des Sommers . . .
During the summer . . .

b. conjunction (verb at end of clause): *while*

Während er zu Hause **war,** . . .
While he was at home . . .

32. was . . . auch: *whatever*

Was er Ihnen **auch** erzählen mag, glauben Sie ihm nicht.
Whatever he may tell you, don't believe him.
Was es **auch** kosten mag, er wird es kaufen.
Whatever it may cost, he will buy it.

Translate:

1. Während er in der Kirche war, brachen Diebe in seine Wohnung ein.
2. Was er auch sagte, man glaubte ihm nicht. 3. Bringen Sie uns bitte
unser Frühstück! 4. Trotzdem ich alles genau so gemacht habe, wie Sie
es mir gesagt haben, startet mein Auto nicht. 5. Bringen Sie uns unser
Frühstück bald, so gebe ich Ihnen ein gutes Trinkgeld. 6. Ich habe alles
genau so getan, wie Sie es mir gesagt haben, und trotzdem startet mein
Auto nicht. 7. Während des Sommers—während des Winters—während
des Vortrages—während der Ferien. 8. Was er auch sagen mag, glauben
Sie ihm nicht! 9. Käme er nur bald! 10. Will er in die Alpen, dann will
sie an die Nordsee.

33. wie

a. question: *how*

Wie alt ist er?
How old is he?

b. exclamation: *how*

Und wie!
And how!

c. comparison

(equality) *as*

Er ist **so alt wie** ich.
He is as old as I.

(similarity) *like*

Sie weinte **wie ein Kind.**
She cried like a child.

34. er will

Avoid *he will:*

Er will nicht mitkommen.
He doesn't want to come along.

35. wohl

a. Wohl is often used with the future and future perfect of probability:
probably, I think, I suppose

Er **wird wohl** nicht **kommen.**
He probably won't come.
Sie **wird** mich heute **wohl** nicht mehr **anrufen.**
I don't think she will call me anymore today.
Er **wird wohl** hier **gewesen sein,** das Licht ist noch an.
He probably was here; the light is still on.

b. wohl implies that a confirmation is expected:

Er hat es **wohl** vergessen.
He forgot it, I suppose.

36. zu and Infinitive: *of* and *-ing* Form

Der Gedanke, sie **zu verlieren,** war ihm unerträglich.
The thought of losing her was unbearable to him.

Translate:

1. Was er wirklich will, ist etwas ganz anderes. 2. Er wird wohl zu Hause

sein, ich sehe Licht.   3. Die Notwendigkeit, hier energisch handeln zu
müssen, sah er wohl nicht ein.   4. Wie viele Personen waren bei der Hochzeit?   5. Habt ihr gut gegessen?—Und wie!   6. Er will ein Gentleman werden.   7. Sie sind wohl auch gegen die neuen Steuern?   8. Manche Dörfer
in Pennsylvania sehen aus wie deutsche Dörfer.   9. Er ist so groß wie sie.
10. Winnipeg, Kanada, liegt auf demselben Breitengrad wie Frankfurt am
Main.   11. Sie wird wohl zu Hause gewesen sein, der Gasherd ist noch
warm.

C. Syntactical Difficulties

1. Object First

For emphasis or variety, Germans frequently begin a sentence with the
object:

Ihn mag ich nicht.
I don't like him.

To retain the emphatic character of this short sentence, we might translate
it by: *He is one I don't like.*

a. The object-first sentence is easily recognized if it begins with an inflected
form of the definite or indefinite article or of a **der**-word or **ein**-word:

Einem Menschen wie deinem Bruder bin ich noch nie begegnet.
I have never met a man like your brother.
Einem Menschen wie meinem Bruder solltest du kein Geld leihen.
You should not lend money to a man like my brother.

b. The object-first construction is more difficult to spot when it begins with
a neuter, feminine, or plural accusative form, since these forms are
identical with their nominatives:

Die französische Küche mag er am liebsten.
He likes French cooking best.

*Translate (subject-first constructions are mixed with object-first construc-
tions):*

1. Keins der Kleider in diesem Laden hat die Farbe, die ich haben möchte.
2. Keins der Kleider in diesem Laden möchte ich haben.   3. Welcher unter
den großen Dichtern der Weltliteratur hat das gesagt?   4. Welchen dieser

großen Dichter kennen Sie? 5. Deine arme Frau solltest du wirklich einmal zum Essen ausführen. 6. Deiner armen Frau kannst du wirklich nicht mehr Arbeit aufbürden; die arbeitet schwer genug. 7. Das Schönste, was wir in Rom gesehen haben, kann ich gar nicht beschreiben. 8. Hunde liebt er, Katzen liebt er, aber um seine Familie kümmert er sich nicht. 9. Ein Haus kannst du in dieser Gegend sehr billig kaufen. 10. Ihn kennst du nicht? Ihn kennt doch jedes Kind in der Nachbarschaft. 11. Das Resultat des Experimentes, obgleich zu Anfang wenig überzeugend, hat man später als den ersten Schritt zur Lösung des Problems angesehen. 12. Den wirklichen Grund für dein langes Schweigen kannst du mir nicht sagen? 13. Eine Reise nach Europa können wir diesen Sommer leider nicht machen. 14. Eine Reise nach Europa würde mich diesen Sommer zu viel Zeit kosten. 15. Kleider machen Schneider, aber viele Mädchen machen ihre eigenen Kleider. 16. Seiner Frau und seinem besten Freunde sagte er nichts von seiner Entdeckung. 17. Die Zauberkraft, die die Märchen auf jung und alt ausüben, haben die Brüder Grimm richtig erkannt. 18. Diesen Idealen ist der Gelehrte sein ganzes Leben lang treu geblieben. 19. Den Geist dieser Zeit zeigt die folgende Bemerkung Hegels. 20. Solche Fragen beantworten Historiker verschieden.

2. Omitted wenn

a. *If I had known that, I would have kept silent.* (or)
Had I known that, I would have kept silent.

In English conditional clauses, "if" may be omitted only if the conditional expresses something contrary to fact. In German, the conditional conjunction **wenn** is frequently omitted in any conditional clause. Compare:

Wenn er nicht bald kommt, so (dann) gehen wir allein ins Kino.
Kommt er nicht bald, so (dann) gehen wir allein ins Kino.
If he doesn't come soon, we'll go to the movie alone.

The conditional without **wenn** starts with the verb. The conclusion is introduced by **so** or **dann.**

b. Compare:

Wir gehen allein ins Kino, **wenn er nicht bald kommt.**
Wir gehen allein ins Kino, **kommt er nicht bald.**

The conditional clause may follow the conclusion. In that case, too, the omitted **wenn** causes a verb-first construction in German.

3. The <u>wenn</u> . . . <u>auch</u> Construction

a. **Wenn** er **auch** nie in Deutschland war, **so** weiß er **doch** mehr von dem Land als mancher Deutschlehrer.

Even though he was never in Germany, he nevertheless knows more about that country than many a teacher of German.

The combination **wenn . . . auch** in the conditional is a literary substitute for clauses introduced by **obgleich, obwohl, trotzdem.** The main clause usually follows with **so** or **so . . . doch.**

b. In the **wenn . . . auch** construction, **wenn** may also be omitted and substituted by a verb-first construction:

War er auch nie in Deutschland, so weiß er doch mehr von dem Land als mancher Deutschlehrer.
Even though he never was in Germany, etc.

Translate:

1. Wenn die Sonne jetzt auch scheint und der Himmel blau ist, so kann es doch morgen regnen. 2. Gab es auch in den Seebädern nicht viel Fleisch, so konnten die Gäste dafür um so mehr frische Fische bekommen. 3. Zu einem Arzt mußt du gehen, willst du wirklich etwas gegen deine Kopfschmerzen tun. 4. Kennt man ihn ein bißchen besser, dann merkt man bald, daß er ein hochgebildeter Mensch ist. 5. Will man etwas Schönes erleben, dann ist es das Beste, diese Gegend zu Pferde zu bereisen. Hat man sich ans Reiten gewöhnt, dann wird dieser Teil der Reise der schönste sein. 6. Wußte man zu Hause auch nichts davon, wie schlecht es ihm ging, so hatten doch seine Mitarbeiter im Laboratorium gemerkt, daß er krank aussah. 7. Hat er uns auch im vorigen Jahr geholfen, so ist es zweifelhaft, ob er uns in diesem Jahr wieder helfen wird, denn er hat geschäftliche Sorgen. 8. Wenn er sich auch sehr schlecht fühlte, so kam er doch jeden Tag zur Arbeit. 9. Das 19. Jahrhundert hat großes Interesse für Goethes Faust gezeigt, wenn es auch das philosophische Werk nicht immer richtig verstand. 10. Sprach er aber zum Direktor über diese Tatsachen, so schüttelte dieser nur den Kopf und wollte nichts davon wissen. 11. Brachte er auch einigen Armen Hilfe, so gab es doch viele andere, die er nicht erreichte. 12. Suchte man ihn, so fand man ihn an seinem Schreibtisch, eifrig schreibend, als wäre nichts geschehen. 13. Hatte man auch die Oper in Prag verstanden, so war das in Wien nicht der Fall. 14. Seine Krankheit hat seine Schaffenskraft nicht beeinflußt, mag das auch paradox klingen. 15. Ist Nürnberg auch heute eine vorwiegend moderne Stadt, so gibt es doch noch immer kleine Straßen, wo man etwas von dem Geist des Mittelalters spürt.

4. Infinitive as Subject

Ihn jetzt **verlassen,** heißt, ihm die Freundschaft kündigen.
To leave him now means to withdraw our friendship.

In German, as in English, the infinitive may be the subject of a sentence. In German, the infinitive stands at the end of the phrase; in English, at the beginning.

Translate:

1. Vernünftig essen, genug schlafen, nicht zuviel rauchen und trinken sind vier ausgezeichnete Gesundheitsregeln. 2. Die Wünsche aller Menschen befriedigen, ist eine Kunst, die keiner kann. 3. In diesem Stadtviertel nachts allein spazierengehen, heißt, das Schicksal herausfordern. 4. Von einer giftigen Schlange in einsamer Gegend, wo es lange dauert, bis man einen Arzt findet, gebissen werden, bedeutet einen langsamen, qualvollen Tod. 5. Ein paar Stunden in der Sonne durch diese hügelige Landschaft wandern, nennst du eine Strapaze? 6. Alles verstehen, heißt, alles verzeihen. 7. Diese Sonate an erster Stelle nennen, heißt, andere wichtige Kompositionen übersehen. 8. Die Krankheit, die zufällig ist und nicht vom Menschen geplant ist, zum herrschenden Einfluß in der Geschichte machen, bedeutet, den Zufall zum Herrscher der Geschichte machen. 9. Von einem armen Manne verlangen, höhere Steuern zu bezahlen, wäre zwecklos. 10. Von den Zeitgenossen eines großen Komponisten erwarten, daß sie ihn mit den Augen der Nachwelt sehen, heißt, vom durchschnittlichen Konzertbesucher das musikalische Verständnis eines Musikkritikers erwarten.

5. Terminal Position of the Infinitive

a. Compare the following German sentence with its English translation:

Daß Zigarettenrauchen sehr ungesund ist, **läßt sich** heute nach den vielen ärztlichen Untersuchungen mit größter Sicherheit **behaupten.**
After the many medical examinations, it can be asserted with greatest certainty today that cigarette smoking is very unhealthy.

In the example given above, the expression **läßt sich** calls for an infinitive. Because of the terminal position of the German infinitive, the phrase "can be asserted" is torn apart: **läßt sich . . . behaupten.**

The terminal position of the infinitive sometimes offers difficulties in reading German expository prose. Before a German sentence can be grasped "at a glance," be aware of words or phrases calling for an infinitive, such as:

er weigert sich . . . zu gehen
he refuses to go . . .
es war ihm unmöglich, uns . . . zu helfen
it was impossible for him to help us . . .

b. In the example under **a,** the position of the infinitive was "conspicuous" because the end of the clause and the end of the sentence were the same. Thus the infinitive appeared before the period. When the end of a clause is *within* a sentence, it may be indicated by a punctuation mark as well as by **und, oder, aber, sondern, als,** as the following examples illustrate:

Daß Zigarettenrauchen sehr ungesund ist, **läßt sich** heute nach den vielen ärztlichen Untersuchungen mit größerer Sicherheit **behaupten.**

Daß Zigarettenrauchen sehr ungesund ist, **läßt sich** heute nach den vielen ärztlichen Untersuchungen mit größerer Sicherheit **behaupten** und wird auch heute von mehr Menschen geglaubt als zu Beginn dieser Untersuchungen.

Daß Zigarettenrauchen sehr ungesund ist, **läßt sich** heute nach den vielen ärztlichen Untersuchungen mit größerer Sicherheit **behaupten** als noch vor zehn Jahren.

Translate:

1. Es war nicht mein Wunsch, dem jungen Menschen so eine schwere Verantwortung aufzubürden. 2. Wir warnten ihn, bei schlechtem Wetter in dem kleinen Segelboot, das außerdem Reparaturen nötig hat, nicht auf den See hinauszufahren. 3. Es war sein Ziel, nach einem halben Jahr Arbeit in der Fabrik seines Bruders seine Studien an der Göttinger Universität fortzusetzen, damit er schließlich mit der Dissertation beginnen könne. 4. Du weißt es ja, daß es immer meine Absicht war, meinen Vater, einen gutherzigen Träumer, aber unpraktischen Geschäftsmann, vor seinem Bruder, seinem brutalsten Konkurrenten, zu warnen und daß ich es nie konnte. 5. Ich habe ihm schon vor zehn Jahren geraten, sich mehr um sein Geschäft und weniger um seine Rennpferde zu kümmern. 6. Hoffentlich hast du nicht vergessen, den Scheck für Dr. Reinicke, dessen Rechnung du mehr als zwei Monate nicht bezahlt hast, mit Luftpost abzuschicken. 7. Er riet ihm, seine fruchtlosen Spekulationen aufzugeben und sich ganz seinem Beruf zu widmen.

6. Present and Past Participles in Participial Phrases

Compare the position of the present and past participles in the following two German sentences with their English equivalents:

Sich immer im Schatten der langen Mauer **haltend,** folgte der Schutzmann dem Einbrecher.
Keeping always in the shadow of the long wall, the policeman followed the burglar.

Durch das Donnern der Brandung und den starken Wind halb **betäubt,** stand er neben dem Fischerboot und träumte.
Half stunned by the thunderous surf and the strong wind, he stood beside the fisherman's boat and dreamed.

Present and past participles in participial phrases stand at the end of the phrase in German, at the beginning of the phrase in English.

Translate:

1. Aus vielen Wunden blutend, lag der Verwundete lange im Schützengraben. 2. Ganz erschöpft und mit schmerzenden Muskeln weiterkämpfend, gelang es ihm dennoch, seinen Gegner zu besiegen. 3. Von Fliegen, Durst und großer Hitze geplagt, arbeiteten die Ochsen stundenlang im Feld. 4. Von der Reklame bis zum Himmel gepriesen und von den besten Musikkritikern begeistert gelobt, begann die Oper, die deutschen Bühnen zu erobern. 5. Vor Schmerz und Wut laut brüllend, raste der verwundete Löwe auf den zitternden Jäger zu. 6. Langsam durch die vielen Seiten der dicken Grammatik blätternd, seufzte er und sagte: „Werde ich diese Sprache je beherrschen?"

7. Parallel Constructions

a. Es gefällt uns nicht, **daß unser Manager** die Pläne für die weitere Entwicklung unserer Firma selber **macht und** sie nur in ganz seltenen Fällen mit seinen Mitarbeitern **bespricht oder** diese nach ihrer Meinung **fragt.**
We dislike it that our manager makes the plans for the further development of our firm himself and discusses them only in very rare cases with his fellow workers or asks these men for their opinion.

In a dependent clause, a finite verb stands last. Ordinarily this position ends the verbal phrase. Before the coordinating conjunctions **und, oder, aber,** however, the verbal phrase does not end but continues.

In sentence (a), the complete verbal phrase is: . . . **unser Manager** . . . **selber macht und** . . . **bespricht** . . . **oder fragt.** Manager is therefore the subject of the two verbals connected by **und** and the third verbal connected by **oder.** The verbs in these three clauses are all governed by **Es gefällt uns nicht, daß** . . . Here, as always, the student must check all terminal positions for verbs and determine where they belong.

b. **Eiweiß und Sahne müssen** gut und lange **geschlagen und** dann zum Gefrieren in den Kühlschrank **gesetzt werden.**
Eggwhites and cream must be beaten well and a long time and then put into the refrigerator for freezing.

In sentence (b), the complete verbal phrase is **Eiweiß und Sahne müssen** . . . **geschlagen und** . . . **gesetzt werden. Eiweiß und Sahne** is the subject of both verbals. The passive auxiliary **werden** at the end of the second verbal also governs the first verbal.

Translate:

1. Niemand wollte uns sagen, ob so ein Experiment gemacht und ob etwas darüber veröffentlicht worden war. 2. Er schickte seinen Eltern ein Telegramm, da er kein Geld mehr hatte und nichts Wertvolles verkaufen wollte, aber seine Miete sofort bezahlen mußte. 3. Er zeigte sich als einer, der für Einzelheiten kein Interesse hat und immer von anderen erwartet, daß sie sich damit beschäftigen. 4. Man behauptete, daß die Entdeckung ein Zufall gewesen sei und von irgend jemand hätte gemacht werden können. 5. Schweitzer wußte, daß er nur einigen Kranken Hilfe bringen und andere, die tief im Urwald lebten, nicht erreichen konnte. 6. Plötzlich wurde es ihm klar, daß er jahrelang nicht an sie gedacht und sogar ihren Namen vergessen hatte. 7. Ich habe ihn immer wieder davor gewarnt, diesem Menschen, den er seinen Freund nennt, etwas von seinen Plänen zu erzählen oder ihn sogar in seiner Firma anzustellen. 8. Er hat uns plötzlich verlassen, ohne einem von uns etwas von seinen Plänen zu sagen oder wenigstens seine vielen Schulden zu bezahlen. 9. Manche Psychologen wollen Freuds Mitarbeiter, Dr. Breuer, neben oder über Freud setzen, womit ein kluger Arzt auf Kosten eines Genies für unsterblich erklärt und so der Mediokrität geschmeichelt wird. 10. Noch heute sind seine Bücher von großer Bedeutung und werden auch im Ausland von Wissenschaftlern gelesen und oft zitiert.

8. Complex Attribute

The German complex attribute is an adjectival or participial phrase that precedes the noun, while its English equivalent follows it. Thus the underlined attribute in **ein über die Stadt fliegendes Flugzeug** is expressed in English by *flying over the city*. Before translating a long (or complex) attribute, you must first be aware that you have encountered such a construction. You can recognize it by the "clash." As you translate **ein über die** (*an over the*), you realize that *an* and *over* clash. You want a noun for the article. This noun is ordinarily preceded by a past or present participle with an adjective ending. The participle is the key word and comes third in the translation. Then follows the rest as the fourth element. It is, however, often better style in English to use a relative clause, rather than a participial phrase.

a. Key word a present participle

Translate the present participle by the active voice:

ein / **über die Stadt fliegendes** Flugzeug

1	4	3	2
(clash)		(key word)	

an airplane flying (*which is flying*) *over the city*

Translate the present participle by the passive voice when the participle is governed by **zu**:

der **zu operierende** Patient
the patient to be operated on
ein leicht **zu lösendes** Problem
a problem that can be solved easily

b. Key word a past participle

Translate a past participle by the passive voice:

das / **in Kalifornien gefundene** Gold

1	4	3	2

the gold (*that was*) *found in California*

c. Key word an adjective

Supply a form of *to be* as the verb of the relative clause (the relative pronoun and the form of *to be* become part of the third element):

Er zeigte uns die / **nur im Röntgenbild sichtbare** Veränderung.

1	4	3	2

He showed us the change, (*which was*) *visible only in the X ray.*

The noun may be modified by an adjective in addition to a complex attribute. Such adjectives must be translated with the noun (2):

ein / **über die Stadt fliegendes** amerikanisches Flugzeug

   1   4   3   2

an American airplane flying over the city.

Translate:

1. Er mußte für die in Bonn lebenden Brüder sorgen. 2. Der aus Wien stammende Musiker wurde von allen verehrt. 3. Es wird unsere Aufgabe sein, die das Problem betreffenden Fragen zu beantworten. 4. Die im 19. Jahrhundert im Mittelpunkt des musikalischen Lebens stehende Pariser Oper tat nichts für Wagner. 5. Diese Frage ist von den auf diesem Gebiet arbeitenden Forschern bis heute nicht beantwortet worden. 6. Er hatte das zu veröffentlichende Manuskript noch nicht beendet. 7. Die sofort zu operierenden verwundeten Soldaten wurden so schnell wie möglich ins Feldlazarett gebracht. 8. Leonardo da Vinci hatte sich schon mit dem erst viel später zu lösenden Problem des menschlichen Fluges beschäftigt. 9. Niemand wollte seine in Köln gemachten Schulden bezahlen. 10. Das war die von Beethoven gewünschte Wirkung. 11. Die vor kurzer Zeit veröffentlichten Untersuchungen genügten, die Theorie zu beweisen. 12. Er wohnte jahrelang in seinem ihm vom König geschenkten Landhause. 13. Das finden Sie in keiner der von Mozart komponierten Opern. 14. Diese nur unter einem Mikroskop sichtbaren Veränderungen erkannte Professor Gerber sofort als die von ihm lang gesuchte Erklärung des sogenannten Schneider-Symptoms. 15. Das schon damals sehr berühmte Wien sollte seine neue Heimat werden. 16. Sie erzählte uns eine für Beethoven sehr charakteristische Episode. 17. Damals komponierte er die jetzt in der ganzen Welt bekannte Sonate. 18. Die Hauptattraktion war der in Wien bekannte und berühmte Pianist Wölfl. 19. Das in etwa zwanzig Meter Tiefe auf dem Meeresboden liegende Unterseeboot war auf der Photographie als ein einem großen Fisch ähnlicher Schatten deutlich zu sehen. 20. Es gibt aber auch ähnliche und darum immer zu den Bakterien gerechnete Formen. 21. Ein in der ganzen Welt berühmt gewordenes Produkt ist der Volkswagen. 22. Gegen die Intrigen der ihn und seine Kunst nicht verstehenden feindlichen Partei konnte sogar der König ihn nicht schützen. 23. Nach zwei in großer Armut in Paris verlebten Jahren ging er wieder nach Deutschland. 24. Die Beobachtungsgabe dieser mit ganz einfachen, manchmal primitiven Instrumenten arbeitenden Forscher muß sehr gut gewesen sein. 25. Dies findet sich in keinem der oben be-

sprochenen Aufsätze.   26. Seine unter günstigen Verhältnissen unter-
nommenen Versuche beweisen das.   27. Aus einem vor kurzer Zeit in der
Zeitschrift „Natur" veröffentlichten Aufsatz zitieren wir das Folgende.
28. Er ließ sich von seiner Sekretärin die von deutschen Geschäftsfreunden
geschickten Briefe übersetzen, um ihre Deutschkenntnisse zu prüfen.

Part Three

Aids for Speaking and Writing

1. Again

a. Repetition without specific reference to a previous occasion: **wieder**

We are here again.
Wir sind **wieder** hier.

I'll never do this again.
Ich tue das nie **wieder.**

I have forgotten your name again.
Ich habe **wieder** Ihren Namen vergessen.

b. Something previously attempted or completed is done once more: **noch einmal**

Let's try again.
Versuchen wir es **noch einmal!**

Let's sing this song again.
Singen wir das Lied **noch einmal!**

c. Idiom: *again and again* = **immer wieder**

Express in German:

1. We are back again. 2. I hope you will visit us again soon. 3. I hope you will visit us again before you leave for Europe. 4. He had to write the letter again. 5. Would you explain this again? 6. Please play the piece again. 7. I'll never speak to (with) him again. 8. Are you smoking again? 9. When will he go to Germany again? 10. I have to write the same letter again. 11. I'll never dance with him again. 12. Say that again. 13. I have lost my hat again. 14. Try it again. 15. He tried it again and again.

2. Another

a. *different:* **ein ander-**

Bring me another glass; this one is cracked.
Bringen Sie mir **ein anderes** Glas; dieses hier hat einen Sprung!

b. *additional:* **noch ein**

Bring us another glass; this gentleman will drink with us.
Bringen Sie uns **noch ein** Glas; dieser Herr wird mit uns trinken!

c. Idioms:

That's another thing.
Das ist **etwas anderes.**

another five years
noch fünf Jahre

one after another
einer nach dem anderen

not another penny
keinen Pfennig mehr

Express in German:

1. Would you like another piece of bread? 2. I'll tell you that another
time. 3. He received one letter after another. 4. Today I received another
letter from him. 5. He is of another opinion. 6. Give him another cup
of coffee. 7. I'll show you another room. 8. Please give me another bar
of soap. 9. Do you have another book like this? 10. I wish we lived in
another house. 11. Would you like another piece of butter? 12. Two are
not enough. I need another piece of paper. 13. Do you want another
cover for your bed? 14. You have two cars; why do you want another?

3. To Ask

a. *to ask a question:* **fragen, eine Frage stellen**

He asked me where I lived.
Er fragte mich, wo ich wohnte.
May I ask a question?
Darf ich eine Frage stellen?

b. *to ask about someone or something; to inquire:* **fragen nach**

She asked me about you.
Sie hat mich nach dir gefragt.
Let's ask about the way.
Fragen wir nach dem Weg!

c. *to ask somebody for something; to request something:* **bitten um**

He asked me for money.
Er hat mich um Geld gebeten.

d. *to demand, expect:* **verlangen**

He asks too much for his car.
Er verlangt zuviel Geld für sein Auto.

e. *to invite, ask out:* **einladen**

He asked me to a dance.
Er hat mich zu einem Tanz **eingeladen.**

f. *to inquire about somebody or something:* **sich nach jemand / etwas erkundigen**

He asked about my health.
Er hat sich nach meiner Gesundheit erkundigt.

g. Idioms:

There is no harm in asking.
Fragen schadet nichts. (or) Man darf doch mal fragen.
He is asking for it.
Er fordert es geradezu heraus.
That is asking too much.
Das ist zuviel verlangt.

Express in German:

1. Why don't you ask him? 2. She asked me for my name. 3. He is asking for his money. 4. Did you ask me something? 5. May I ask you for a light (Feuer)? 6. He asked me for dinner. 7. She asked me the same question. 8. They ask 10 dollars for that. 9. He asked me to show him my passport. 10. He asked for a raise. 11. He asked about my sister. 12. He asked me for my address. 13. He asked permission to leave. 14. I hope she will ask me to tea. 15. He asked me: "Where is the bank?" 16. Did you ask him for his opinion? 17. Ask him for the way to the post office. 18. Ask him for the price of the room again. 19. I ask myself why I did it. 20. Why don't you ask him for advice? 21. Did anybody ask for me? 22. He asked them on his knees. 23. I would like to ask you not to be late. 24. How much does he ask for the car? 25. That is asking too much. 26. He asked me to go with him to the theater. 27. The grandmother asked what the name of the baby was. 28. He asked me to stay a little longer. 29. He asked me what he should do. 30. I'll ask him where the post office is. 31. The child asked her mother for a piece of chocolate. 32. You are asking too much money for your house. 33. The mother asked many children to the birthday party. 34. We had to ask in the hospital about his room number. 35. When she is asked how old she is, she blushes.

4. To Change

a. *to make different, alter:* **ändern**

My mother altered this dress.
Meine Mutter hat dieses Kleid geändert.

b. *to become different, alter in appearance:* **sich verändern**

He has changed since the accident.
Seit dem Unfall **hat er sich verändert.**
Nothing has changed here.
Hier **hat sich nichts verändert.**

c. *to substitute one thing for another; to give or get smaller money in exchange:* **wechseln**

Would you like to change places?
Möchten Sie **die Plätze wechseln?**
Can you change a dollar?
Können Sie **einen Dollar wechseln?**

d. *to change one currency for another:* **umwechseln**

I would like to change 10 dollars into marks.
Ich möchte **10 Dollar gegen DM umwechseln.**

e. *to change one's clothes:* **sich umziehen**

I have to change for dinner.
Ich muß mich für das Abendessen **umziehen.**

f. *to change trains:* **umsteigen**

You must change trains in Cologne.
Sie müssen **in Köln umsteigen.**

g. Idiom:

I have changed my mind.
Ich habe mir's anders überlegt.

Express in German:

1. Don't change the title of your dissertation.   2. He has changed a little.
3. I must change my American money.   4. Can you change five dollars?
5. She has changed her opinion.   6. He has changed to his advantage.
7. The airplane changed (the) direction.   8. I would like to change a mark.
9. You will have to change before you go out.   10. He changed into the
wrong train.   11. If you go by bus, you won't have to change.   12. She has
changed her mind.   13. She changed her plans again.   14. We didn't
change places.   15. Why don't you change your money in Berlin?
16. Where can I change American money?   17. The butcher changes his
prices every day.   18. There is no direct connection; you will have to
change.   19. If you change your name, you will also change your character.
20. He changes friends as easily as people change (their) cars.

5. To Enjoy

a. *to experience with joy:* **genießen**

We enjoyed the cool air after the thunderstorm.
Wir genossen die kühle Luft nach dem Gewitter.

b. *to enjoy oneself; to have a good time:* **sich amüsieren**

I had a wonderful time in the cabaret last night.
Ich habe mich gestern abend im Kabarett wunderbar **amüsiert.**

c. when the object of enjoyment is food, drink, or smoke: **schmecken**

Do you enjoy German cooking?
Schmeckt Ihnen die deutsche Küche?

d. when the enjoyment is derived from an aesthetic pleasure: **gefallen**

How did you enjoy the German performance of Much Ado about Nothing?
Wie hat Ihnen die deutsche Aufführung von *Viel Lärm um nichts* **gefallen?**

e. *to like to do something:* **etwas gerne tun**

I enjoy skiing, but my wife prefers skating.
Ich **laufe gern** Ski, aber meine Frau **läuft lieber** Schlittschuh.

f. *it gives me pleasure, it is fun for me,* followed by the *-ing* form of the verb in English but by the infinitive in German: **Es macht mir Freude. Es macht mir Spaß** is used for less solemn situations:

I enjoy hearing Beethoven again.
Es macht mir Freude, Beethoven wieder **zu hören.**
My children enjoy playing in the rain.
Es macht meinen Kindern Spaß, im Regen **zu spielen.**

Express in German:

1. He enjoys his life. 2. I have enjoyed this walk. 3. I enjoyed the concert. 4. He did not enjoy his cigar; he must be sick. 5. I can't enjoy myself at (auf) his parties. 6. How did you enjoy Paris in the spring? 7. How did you enjoy the play last night? 8. I enjoy Moselwein more than Rheinwein. 9. I enjoy being again with my German friends. 10. I enjoy walking barefoot in the wet grass. 11. Enjoy (the) life while you are young. 12. I enjoy sleeping late (lange). 13. I enjoy playing table tennis, but my brother prefers playing American football. 14. I enjoyed reading the interesting article about Rilke. 15. I enjoyed meeting you.

6. To Feel

a. *to perceive or examine by touch; to feel something like pain or joy or any other sensation or emotion:* **fühlen**

Just feel how cold my hands are.
Fühl mal, wie kalt meine Hände sind!
I feel a pressure in my chest.
Ich fühle einen Druck in der Brust.

b. definite pains are expressed by **Schmerzen haben**

I feel pains in my arms and in the chest when I walk fast.
Ich habe Schmerzen in den Armen und in der Brust, wenn ich schnell gehe.

c. referring to physical or mental conditions: **sich fühlen**

How do you feel?
Wie fühlen Sie sich?
I feel good (bad).
Ich fühle mich wohl (unwohl).

d. *to suspect something; to have a physical or mental premonition or suspicion:* **ich habe das Gefühl, [als (ob)]; mir ist, als (ob)**

I feel (as if) it is going to rain.
Ich habe das Gefühl, es wird regnen.
I felt as if another person were in my room.
Ich hatte das Gefühl, als wäre noch jemand in meinem Zimmer.
Mir war, als ob noch jemand in meinem Zimmer wäre.

e. Idioms:

I feel cold (hot).
Mir ist kalt (heiß).
I feel sorry for him.
Er tut mir leid.
I feel sure.
Ich bin überzeugt.
I feel it my duty to tell you.
Ich halte es für meine Pflicht, Ihnen das zu sagen.

Express in German:

1. I didn't feel anything. 2. I feel he doesn't want to do it. 3. I can't feel his pulse. 4. I felt firm ground under my feet. 5. She feels better. 6. He felt as if this was the turning point in his life. 7. I feel something hard. 8. I feel he won't come back so soon. 9. I feel it my duty to help him. 10. I feel my heart beat. 11. I felt that someone was behind me. 12. You

mustn't feel as a stranger. 13. She feels unhappy. 14. I feel not responsible for his actions. 15. He feels unsure. 16. I feel that I am doing the right thing. 17. I hardly felt the pain. 18. She felt the loss very deeply. 19. I felt as if this meant the end of our friendship. 20. When I'm tired I feel pain(s) everywhere. 21. He doesn't feel as well today as he felt yesterday. 22. After the rain I could feel the moisture in the air. 23. I feel much better today.

7. To Get

a. *to become:* **werden**

> *It's getting very hot.*
> **Es wird sehr heiß.**

b. *to receive; to come into possession of:* **bekommen;** colloquial **kriegen**

> *I got a letter.*
> **Ich habe** einen Brief **bekommen (gekriegt).**

c. same as b; implies greater distance: **erhalten**

> *I got your package from Italy.*
> **Ich habe** dein Paket aus Italien **erhalten.**

d. *to obtain;* suggests putting forth effort: **verschaffen**

> *Can you get me a room?*
> **Können Sie** mir ein Zimmer **verschaffen?**

e. suggests buying, hiring, or procuring: **besorgen**

> *Can you get me a ticket?*
> **Können Sie** mir eine Theaterkarte **besorgen?**

f. *to go and fetch:* **holen**

> *Get me a glass of water, please.*
> **Holen Sie** mir bitte ein Glas Wasser!

Express in German:

1. What did you get for Christmas? 2. Get me my hat, please. 3. It got very cold. 4. We got rain last night. 5. I got very tired. 6. Why did he get angry? 7. He gets money for it. 8. How did he get this money? 9. I have to get a ticket for my brother, too. 10. I have to get her trunk from the station. 11. The days are getting longer now. 12. I didn't get an answer yet. 13. Would you get me a taxi, please? 14. She got red.

15. Did you get good news from home? 16. Would you get me some cigarettes? 17. Please get the bread from the kitchen. 18. Please get me a glass of water. 19. The milk got sour. 20. She got another present from him. 21. I got your letter yesterday. 22. Did you get the mail from the post office? 23. They don't have the book in this store. I'll ask the owner to get one for me. 24. He got the books he ordered. 25. You will have to get the tickets. I have no time. 26. If you get the money, I'll get the ticket. 27. I can get you a cheaper car.

8. Hard

a. the opposite of soft: **hart**

This bread is too hard.
Dieses Brot ist **zu hart.**

b. *difficult:* **schwierig**

That is a hard question.
Das ist **eine schwierige Frage.**

c. *strenuous; hard to take:* **schwer**

This kind of work is too hard for you.
Diese Art Arbeit ist **zu schwer** für dich.
This is a hard loss.
Dies ist **ein schwerer Verlust.**

d. *vigorously:* **stark**

It snowed very hard.
Es hat **stark** geschneit.

e. Idioms:

This is hard to believe.
Das ist kaum zu glauben.
You must work harder.
Sie müssen mehr arbeiten.

Express in German:

1. He breathed hard. 2. It rained so hard that we could not go. 3. That is hard to say. 4. They have very hard water here. 5. This isn't hard work. 6. This chair is too hard. 7. This is a hard experiment. 8. We have a hard

winter. 9. We had a hard winter last year. 10. It's very hard to get along with him. 11. A diamond is harder than glass. 12. This is a hard life. 13. The bread is hard as stone. 14. She takes everything so hard. 15. This was a hard blow.

9. Idea

a. *thought:* **die Idee**

> *That's a good idea.*
> Das ist **eine gute Idee.**

b. *notion, knowledge:* **die Ahnung**

> *Do you have any idea what this might be?*
> **Haben Sie eine Ahnung,** was das sein könnte?

c. *conception:* **der Begriff**

> *You have no idea how happy he was.*
> **Sie machen sich keinen Begriff** davon, wie glücklich er war.

Express in German:

1. That is a crazy idea. 2. Do you have any idea where that road leads to? 3. I haven't the slightest idea what you mean. 4. Was it your idea to invite this man? 5. That is not a bad idea. 6. I don't have a clear idea about what he wants. 7. I have no idea where he is. 8. I have an idea for a new novel. 9. I have no idea how late it is. 10. Do you have any idea when he will be back? 11. Do you have any idea where I can find him? 12. It was a good idea to burn the letter.

10. To Imagine

a. *to picture to oneself:* **sich vorstellen**

> *Can you imagine that?*
> **Können Sie sich das vorstellen?**

b. *to have an idea, imagine:* **vermuten**

> *I imagine he married into a rich family.*
> **Ich vermute,** er hat in eine reiche Familie geheiratet.

c. to have wrong ideas about oneself, others, the world: **sich einbilden**

> *He imagines that he knows everything better.*
> **Er bildet sich ein,** alles besser zu wissen.

d. Idiom:

> *Just imagine!*
> **Denken Sie nur!**

Express in German:

1. Imagine that you were rich.   2. Just imagine, he won 100 dollars.
3. He often imagines that he is rich.   4. She imagined that somebody
followed her.   5. I imagined him to be a tall, slender person.   6. I can
imagine very well what he said.   7. I imagine that this is much harder than
it looks.   8. I can't imagine why he did that.   9. Just imagine, you are
going to be in Europe in the morning.   10. He imagines he knows everything.   11. Just imagine, the boy won a trip to Germany.   12. Don't
imagine that you are better than other people.   13. I imagine it was he.
14. I have an idea she can't do it.   15. I can't imagine him as a salesman.

11. To Know

a. followed by a clause: **wissen**

> *I know (that) he is here.*
> **Ich weiß, daß er hier ist.**
> **Ich weiß, er ist hier.**

b. *to have knowledge of; to be informed about:* **wissen**

> *He knows everything.*
> **Er weiß alles.**

c. *to be acquainted with* (a person, place, or thing): **kennen**

> *I know such a man.*
> **Ich kenne so einen Mann.**
> *Do you know Berlin?*
> **Kennen Sie Berlin?**
> *Do you know the Old Museum in Berlin?*
> **Kennen Sie das Alte Museum** in Berlin?

d. *to know how to do something:* **können**

> *Do you know how to swim?*
> **Können Sie schwimmen?**

e. to have an understanding of complex matters in fields of learning, institutions, arts, etc.: **verstehen**

I know nothing about music.
Ich verstehe nichts von Musik.

f. Idioms:

She knows the poem by heart.
Sie kann das Gedicht auswendig.
I know German.
Ich kann Deutsch.
Not that I know.
Nicht daß ich wüßte.

Express in German:

1. If I had only known that he was ill. 2. Do you know the book? 3. He knows German and French. 4. I want to know where he is. 5. I know that he knows you. 6. I know Mann's *Magic Mountain*. 7. Do you know where he is? 8. I don't know what he wants. 9. Do you know what to do (was du tun sollst)? 10. He knows everything better. 11. She knows how to cook well. 12. She knows everything. 13. Every child knows the way there. 14. Do you know a good restaurant? 15. Do you know his father? 16. He knows a good remedy for (gegen) it. 17. She knows Paris well. 18. He knows how to convince people. 19. I know him as a reliable man. 20. I don't know that anymore. 21. He knows his trade. 22. As if I didn't know that. 23. I should have known that. 24. I don't know Heine's poems well. 25. Do you know his name? 26. He knows my father very well. 27. How should I know that? 28. I only know that he lived here ten years ago. 29. I didn't know you were ill. 30. Do you know Russian? 31. You may come along if you know how to play football. 32. She knows much about German literature but she doesn't know enough German to order a glass of water. 33. How is it possible that you know so little about music? 34. I don't know the rules. 35. I know the answer by heart. 36. Here is a man who knows something about medicine. 37. I know nothing about philosophy.

12. To Last

a. *to have a certain duration, take a certain time:* **dauern**

How long did the performance last?
Wie lange hat die Vorstellung gedauert?

b. *to be enough:* **ausreichen**

The money will not last for the trip.
Das Geld wird für die Reise **nicht ausreichen.**

c. *to keep fresh:* **sich halten**

The flowers lasted a long time.
Die Blumen haben sich lange **gehalten.**

Express in German:

1. The roses did not last long. 2. Our friendship lasted only for a year.
3. The play was boring and lasted too long. 4. How long, do you think,
will the war last? 5. The coffee won't last. 6. The meeting will last at
least another hour. 7. The class lasts 50 minutes. 8. My salary doesn't
last beyond the 15th of the month. 9. The cake will last if you put it in the
refrigerator. 10. The picture lasted so long that I fell asleep. 11. The test
will last only one hour. 12. I need more money. This won't last another
week.

13. To Learn

a. *to acquire knowledge or ability:* **lernen**

Where did you learn German?
Wo haben Sie Deutsch gelernt?

b. *to receive information:* **hören / erfahren**

I have just learned that you were ill.
Ich habe eben gehört / erfahren, daß Sie krank waren.

Express in German:

1. He learned German from his grandmother. 2. She never learned to
write well. 3. They learned their lesson well. 4. What did you learn in
school today? 5. I learned you are not interested in her. 6. All I learned
was that he lives no longer in Berlin. 7. I learned it once, but now I have
forgotten it again. 8. I learned only now that we have an examination
today. 9. This winter I learned skiing. 10. We learn in the school of life.
11. When she arrived she learned what had happened. 12. When did you
learn to swim?

14. To Leave

TRANSITIVE:

a. *to leave behind; to leave unchanged:* **lassen**

> *I left my keys at home.*
> **Ich habe meine Schlüssel zu Hause gelassen.**
> *I left the door open.*
> **Ich habe die Tür offen gelassen.**

b. *to go away from:* **verlassen**

> *He left the house very early.*
> **Er hat das Haus** sehr früh **verlassen.**

c. *to leave behind after death:* **hinterlassen**

> *He left nothing but debts.*
> **Er hat nichts als Schulden hinterlassen.**

d. *to let lie:* **liegenlassen**

> *I left a book in the classroom.*
> **Ich habe ein Buch** im Klassenzimmer **liegenlassen.**

e. *to leave a task to* another person: **überlassen**

> *I leave it to you to invite her.*
> **Ich überlasse es Ihnen,** sie einzuladen.

INTRANSITIVE:

f. *to leave; to depart:* **gehen / abfahren**

> *We have to leave now.*
> **Wir müssen** jetzt **gehen.**
> *The train will leave in two minutes.*
> **Der Zug fährt** in zwei Minuten **ab.**

g. *to depart, leave* by means of transportation: **fahren**

> *We leave for Europe next week.*
> **Wir fahren** nächste Woche nach Europa.

h. Idiom:

> *Leave me alone.*
> **Laß mich in Ruhe!**

Express in German:

1. He left the office at 8 o'clock. 2. Leave that to me. 3. He left this morning for Paris. 4. I left him in his hotel room. 5. I left plenty of work for you. 6. He leaves a widow and two children. 7. When do you leave? 8. He can't leave the house. 9. He left neither money nor a house. 10. Leave it to me. 11. I couldn't do my homework because I had left my book in school. 12. When will you leave Chicago and return to New York? 13. His aunt did not leave him any money. 14. I was sad when I left Frankfurt. 15. The mother left her children many beautiful memories. 16. Come Heidi, we must leave now. 17. This train always leaves on time. 18. He left it to me to wash the dishes. 19. I left my umbrella in the restaurant. 20. We'll have to leave after this song. 21. On Wednesday I must leave the office ten minutes early because I have an appointment. 22. Leave him alone! 23. Leave everything as it is. 24. He left me without saying a word. 25. You can leave your coat here. 26. She left the house at 10 o'clock. 27. Your train has just left. 28. He left without saying good-by to us. 29. He left his collection to the museum. 30. I leave the selection to you.

15. To Like

a. to have friendly feelings for a person or thing: **mögen, gern haben**

> *I like you, Jürgen, but I don't love you.*
> **Ich mag dich,** Jürgen, aber ich liebe dich nicht.
> **Ich habe dich gern,** Jürgen, aber ich liebe dich nicht.

b. polite expression of wish: *I would like (to have), I would like to do:* **ich möchte**

> *Waiter! I would like a second portion of dessert.*
> Ober! **Ich möchte eine zweite Portion Nachtisch.**
> *We would like to eat now if it is all right with you.*
> **Wir möchten jetzt essen,** wenn es Ihnen recht ist.

c. *to like* to do something: verb + **gern**

> *She likes to dance.*
> **Sie tanzt gern.**

d. *to like to eat* or *drink* something: verb + **gern** (the verb is often understood in English)

> *Do you like spinach?*
> **Essen Sie Spinat gern?**

She likes milk better.
Sie trinkt Milch lieber.

e. to find aesthetic pleasure in: **gefallen**

I like this painting.
Dieses Gemälde gefällt mir.

Express in German:

1. How do you like my new dress? 2. I would like to go to the movies tonight. 3. I like modern music. 4. I like to get up early in the morning. 5. We didn't like the film at all. 6. He likes to eat bread and cheese. 7. He would like to become an official, but he doesn't like responsibility. 8. He likes the suit, but he doesn't have enough money to buy it. 9. If you try it, you will like skating. 10. Most girls like him. 11. Do you like his new blue VW? 12. She doesn't like me. 13. They liked Berlin better than Hamburg. 14. Don't you like sauerbraten? 15. I like Wiener schnitzel better. 16. I like to take a walk after dinner. 17. He doesn't like to fly. 18. I don't like the picture. 19. Don't you like fish? 20. He doesn't like this hospital.

16. To Live

a. *to be alive; to spend one's life in a certain place:* **leben**

Does your father still live?
Lebt Ihr Vater noch?
My parents live in Germany.
Meine Eltern leben in Deutschland.

b. *to dwell:* **wohnen**

Do you still live on Schiller Street? —No, I live again with my parents on Beethoven Boulevard.
Wohnen Sie noch **in der Schillerstraße?** —Nein, **ich wohne** wieder **bei meinen Eltern** in der Beethovenallee.

c. a temporary stay: **sein**

When I am in New York, I always stay with friends.
Wenn ich in New York **bin,** wohne ich immer bei Freunden.

d. Idioms:

Live and learn.
Man lernt nie aus.
Live and let live.
Leben und leben lassen.

Express in German:

1. He lives in the vicinity of our hotel. 2. His daughter lives in America. She married an American. 3. He lived only a few months in our house. 4. If you want to, you can live with my parents. 5. When he lives in Berlin for a few weeks, he always visits us. 6. What kind of life is that! You live a week in Frankfurt, then two weeks in New York, then a few days in Cologne; you never have time for your wife and children. 7. We have been living in this part of (the) town for ten years. 8. These fish live only in tropical waters. 9. He lives in the country. 10. He can only live in America. 11. Three years ago I lived in Bonn. 12. Because of the fire we live in a hotel. 13. He lived in Paris for three years. 14. Live and let live is the motto of his life. 15. He lived only a few weeks longer than his wife.

17. To Meet

a. *to meet by appointment:* **treffen, sich treffen**

I am supposed to meet him at three o'clock.
Ich soll ihn um drei Uhr treffen.
We always meet in front of the library.
Wir treffen uns immer **vor der Bibliothek.**

b. *to meet by chance; to run into:* **begegnen, sich begegnen**

I met the two on the street.
Ich bin den beiden auf der Straße **begegnet.**
I met him in the office of the American Express in Munich.
Ich bin ihm im Büro des American Express in München **begegnet.**

c. *to make the acquaintance of:* **kennenlernen**

They met on a plane.
Sie haben sich in einem Flugzeug **kennengelernt.**

d. Idioms:

I would like you to meet Mr. Schönborn.
Ich möchte Ihnen Herrn Schönborn vorstellen.
Meet Mr. Schönborn.
Dies ist Herr Schönborn.
Pleased to meet you.
Es freut mich, Ihre Bekanntschaft zu machen.

Express in German:

1. I met him at two o'clock. 2. Where shall we meet each other? 3. You

will meet all your old friends there.   4. How did they finally meet?   5. I just met your sister at the corner.   6. Have you met Mr. Brown?   7. We met on the street.   8. I would like you to meet a very good friend of mine. 9. Pleased to have met you.   10. We met at the station.   11. I would like to meet him.   12. I met an old schoolmate in the theater.   13. I would like you to meet my parents.   14. Where did you two meet?

18. Narrow

a. opposite of broad, wide: **schmal**

He has narrow shoulders.
Er hat **schmale Schultern.**

b. *tight, close, confining:* **eng**

Before us lay a narrow valley.
Vor uns lag **ein enges Tal.**
I can swallow pills only with water. My throat is too narrow.
Ich kann Pillen nur mit Wasser schlucken. **Mein Hals ist zu eng.**

Express in German:

1. This bridge is too narrow for your big car.   2. This ribbon is too narrow. 3. The new bookshelf she bought is too narrow.   4. The tower had six narrow windows.   5. We could not carry the piano through the door; it was too narrow.   6. He has narrow hands with long, slender fingers. 7. We walked for hours through the narrow streets of Rothenburg.   8. I'll never forget these fanatical eyes in the narrow face.   9. He escaped through a narrow corridor.   10. These shoes are too tight for my feet.

19. Number

a. *numeral, digit:* **die Zahl**

You must add these numbers.
Sie müssen **diese Zahlen** zusammenzählen.

b. a quantity of individuals or objects: **die Anzahl**

A number of young colleagues were not present.
Eine Anzahl junger Kollegen waren nicht anwesend.

c. one of a series; a number assigned to something: **die Nummer**

The number of his room is 12.
Seine Zimmernummer ist 12.

d. Idioms:

> *a great number*
> **sehr viele**
> *a number of times*
> **einige Male**

Express in German:

1. A number of books were not sold. 2. A great number of members had appeared. 3. The number of participants is too large. 4. I don't know the exact number of participants. 5. Which number have you chosen? 6. What is your telephone number? 7. You will find the information in catalogue number 2. 8. A great number of passengers swam to the shore. 9. He has a great number of good friends. 10. I don't know the exact number of children in these three families. 11. The number of students in this class is limited. 12. Car number 2 won the race. 13. Take car number 8. 14. I saw him a number of times last summer. 15. Check the number. 16. The number of members in our club is not large.

20. To Pass

a. *help a person to a thing; to hand:* **reichen**

> *Please pass the salt.*
> **Bitte reichen Sie mir das Salz!**

b. referring to time: **vergehen**

> *Time passes very slowly for him.*
> **Die Zeit vergeht sehr langsam** für ihn.

c. *to go / drive by* (something): **vorbeigehen / vorbeifahren**

> *I passed your house last night.*
> **Ich bin** gestern abend an Ihrem Haus **vorbeigegangen.**

d. *to undergo successfully* (an examination): **bestehen**

> *She didn't pass the examination.*
> **Sie hat die Prüfung nicht bestanden.**

Express in German:

1. We passed the church. 2. Time passes quickly. 3. Hours have passed. 4. Did you see who was passing? 5. Please read this and pass it to your neighbor. 6. How quickly the time passed! 7. After she had passed the

examination, she flew to Europe. 8. The evening passed very quickly.
9. He passed the first part of the examination. 10. Please pass her the
bread. 11. He passed me without saying a word.

21. People

a. *human beings:* **die Menschen**

> *He likes people.*
> Er liebt **Menschen.**

b. group or class of people: **die Leute**

> *He hates people who brag.*
> Er haßt **Leute, die prahlen.**
> *They are simple people from the country.*
> Es sind **einfache Leute vom Lande.**

c. national unit: **das Volk**

> *The German people has always shown great interest in music.*
> Das deutsche Volk hat immer großes Interesse für Musik **gezeigt.**

d. the common people: **das Volk**

> *He was not an aristocrat but a man of the people.*
> Er war kein Aristokrat, sondern **ein Mann des Volkes.**

Express in German:

1. The people in the theater were very quiet. 2. Only few lions kill people.
3. There were 300 people present. 4. English- and German-speaking people love Hemingway's works. 5. Tell your people (they should) to go
home. 6. Our people have been singing such songs for centuries. 7. The
ancient Homer said: People's voice—God's voice. 8. Old people don't
always understand the young. 9. The people who work for us must know
something about mathematics. 10. It is a mistake to say: All people want
a quiet, secure life. 11. The people may (can) say what they want.
12. Goethe loved the people in (the) villages and small towns. 13. Martin
Luther used the language of the people in his German translation of the
Bible. 14. Do you know how hard our people have worked? 15. I'll talk
to our people about that program. 16. He talked to the American people,
and the people believed him. 17. Not all peoples understand what a modern war means. 18. The people took over the government. 19. They
always forget the poor people. 20. There were many people in the bus; I
could not sit down.

22. To Put

a. *to put* something so that it lies; *to lay:* **legen**

Put the flowers on the table (the flowers are to lie loosely on the table).
Legen Sie die Blumen auf den Tisch!

b. *to put* something so that it stands: **stellen**

Put the flowers on the table (the flowers stand in a vase).
Stellen Sie die Blumen auf den Tisch!

c. to cause a person to sit: **setzen**

Put the child on this chair.
Setzen Sie das Kind auf diesen Stuhl!

d. *to stick* an object into the ground, a slot, the pocket, etc.: **stecken**

He put the pole into the ground.
Er steckte den Pfahl in die Erde.
Put the little package into the mailbox.
Stecken Sie das Päckchen in den Briefkasten!

Express in German:

1. Put the pipe on the ground. 2. Put the pipe in the corner. 3. Put the fish on the kitchen table; here is the knife. 4. Put the fish on the table; we are ready to eat. 5. Don't put money into the machine; it's empty. 6. Don't put your hands in your pockets when you speak with him. 7. Don't put money into the vending machine; it doesn't work. 8. Put your umbrella in the corner. 9. Don't put your wet umbrella on the bed. 10. Put the book on the table. 11. Put the book on the bookshelf. 12. Don't put too much in your briefcase. 13. He put the ring on her finger. 14. Put the lamp on the table. 15. Put the key in my pocket. 16. Put some water on the table. 17. He put a cigar in his mouth. 18. Put the letter in the mailbox. 19. She put the pencil behind her ear. 20. When girls clean up their room, they put their shoes under the bed. 21. Where did you put my coat? 22. Where should I put the vase? 23. She put fifteen candles on the cake. 24. She never puts any money in her bag. 25. Put the salt on the table. 26. Don't put your briefcase on the piano. 27. She put the pencil in her hair. 28. Put the money in your handbag. 29. Put the ladder against the house. 30. Put the baby on the bed. 31. He put his hand on my shoulder. 32. Put the chairs around the table. 33. Put the milk in the refrigerator. 34. You did not put all the books on the bookshelf. 35. You can put your motorcycle in my garage. 36. He puts a flower in his buttonhole every morning. 37. Don't put it in your mouth.

23. To See

a. *to see* in the literal sense: **sehen**

> *It is too dark here; I can't see anything.*
> Es ist zu dunkel hier, **ich kann nichts sehen.**

b. *to understand; to become aware of:* **sehen, verstehen**

> *I see that I have made a mistake.*
> **Ich sehe, daß ich einen Fehler gemacht habe.**
> *Do you see now how it works?*
> **Verstehst du** jetzt, **wie es funktioniert?**

c. *to understand; to see* after previous difficulties or disagreement: **einsehen**

> *Don't you see that you are wrong?*
> **Siehst du nicht ein,** daß du unrecht hast?

d. *to ascertain, learn, find out:* **nachsehen**

> *See if there is any mail.*
> **Sehen Sie nach,** ob die Post da ist!

e. Idioms:

> *I see.* (interjection) *You want to go alone.*
> **Ich verstehe!** Du willst allein gehen.
> *I see.* (surprise) *He wasn't serious*
> **Ach so!** Er hat es nicht ernst gemeint.
> *See to it that you come home on time.*
> **Sieh zu,** daß du rechtzeitig nach Hause kommst!
> *What do you see in her?*
> **Was findest du an ihr?**
> *May I see Mr. Miller?*
> **Kann ich Herrn Miller sprechen?**
> *I'll see you home.*
> **Ich begleite Sie nach Hause.**

Express in German:

1. See who it is. 2. See to it that he finishes the work. 3. He saw that it was too difficult for him. 4. I can't see why he didn't do it. 5. I'll see if the train has arrived. 6. I see you have bought a new car. 7. Let's see if he has finished. 8. See what the word means. 9. I don't see why he didn't give me an "A." 10. See if it's raining. 11. I must see if he closed the house. 12. See that it's done. 13. See who is at the door. 14. She doesn't see very well. 15. For more information, see page 20. 16. Can you see the stage? 17. Have you seen this film? 18. I see everything is in

order here. 19. I'll see what I can do for you. 20. We don't see much
of you anymore. 21. I see my error. 22. Can't you see that he is ill?
23. Can't you see that he is lying? 24. Do you see what I mean? 25. I'll
see if I have it. 26. See where the children are. 27. I see. You deny it.
28. Do you want to see my husband?

24. To Spend

a. *to pay out, dispose of* money: **ausgeben**

> *I have spent too much on it.*
> **Ich habe zuviel dafür ausgegeben.**

b. *to pass time* in a particular manner or place: **verbringen**

> *I spent all day writing letters.*
> **Ich verbrachte den ganzen Tag mit Briefeschreiben.**

Express in German:

1. He spends much money on her. 2. We spent the evening at home.
3. You spent more money for a used car than I for a new one. 4. We
spent the whole day at my aunt's. 5. He spent all his money. 6. Where
did you spend your vacation?

25. To Take

a. *to get into possession of; to select; to use* a vehicle for transportation:
nehmen

> *Take another piece.*
> **Nehmen Sie noch ein Stück!**
> *Take the train / bus / airplane.*
> **Nehmen Sie den Zug / den Bus / das Flugzeug!**

b. *to take* someone or something somewhere: **bringen / begleiten** (a person)

> *Take this letter to the post office.*
> **Bringen Sie diesen Brief zur Post!**
> *He took me home.*
> **Er hat mich nach Hause begleitet.**

c. *to take time, last:* **dauern / brauchen**

> *The trip took two days.*
> **Die Reise hat zwei Tage gedauert.**

It took me exactly one hour.
Ich habe genau eine Stunde dazu **gebraucht.**

d. Idioms:

> *He took a trip.*
> **Er machte eine Reise.**
> *Take my advice.*
> **Folgen Sie meinem Rat!**

Express in German:

1. He took her home. 2. Take me to the Hotel Europe. 3. It took him another hour. 4. Will you take me to the station? 5. He did not take a train. 6. It took us a long time to find him. 7. This takes too long for me. 8. Take your lunch with you. 9. He took me by the hand. 10. It will take only a few minutes. 11. Let's take this road. 12. He took it into his hand. 13. He didn't take a second glass of wine. 14. Why don't you take my car? 15. Take a taxi. 16. We took her to the station. 17. Would you take this chair to the next room? 18. They took him to the hospital. 19. It took him two weeks to paint the house. 20. You should take your money to the bank. 21. It took him all day to write the letter.

26. To Taste

a. *to taste* in the literal sense but only intransitive: **schmecken (nach)**

> *The food tastes especially good today.*
> **Das Essen schmeckt** heute **besonders gut.**
> *The soup tastes of onions.*
> **Die Suppe schmeckt nach Zwiebeln.**

b. *to try the flavor or quality, taste a sample:* **kosten / probieren / versuchen**

> *Taste the soup before you salt it.*
> **Kosten Sie** erst **die Suppe,** bevor Sie sie salzen!
> *You must taste this sausage.*
> **Sie müssen diese Wurst** mal **kosten / probieren / versuchen.**

c. Idiom:

> *This tastes good.*
> **Das schmeckt!**

Express in German:

1. The meat tastes bad. 2. The water tastes of chlorine. 3. I tasted the salad. It tastes like chicken salad. 4. This tastes too sweet for me. 5. This

tastes of soap. 6. I have never tasted this before. 7. Do you taste the wine in this sauce? 8. Did you taste the soup? 9. I don't taste a thing. 10. The butter tastes of onion.

27. To Tell

a. *to relate a story; to give an account of:* **erzählen**

> *Tell us something about your trip.*
> **Erzählen Sie uns etwas von Ihrer Reise!**

b. *to say; to inform* a person; *to order or command:* **sagen** (with **sollen**)

> *Tell him not to be (he should not be) late.*
> **Sagen Sie ihm,** daß er nicht zu spät kommen soll!

c. Idioms:

> *You can't tell him anything.*
> **Er läßt sich nichts sagen.**
> *I told you so.*
> **Ich habe es dir ja gleich gesagt.**
> *You can hardly tell the difference between them.*
> **Die beiden kann man kaum unterscheiden.**
> *I'll tell you what.*
> **Ich will dir was sagen.**

Express in German:

1. Tell me the truth. 2. I'll tell you what I want. 3. Tell us of your experiences in Germany. 4. I can tell you it's not easy. 5. He told us a true story. 6. Tell him what happened to you last night. 7. Tell me where you were. 8. Tell me how it happened. 9. You can tell that to your grandmother. 10. He told you the truth. 11. Can you tell us this story in German? 12. He told me much about you. 13. I told you I didn't want to be disturbed. 14. Tell him to go home. 15. Tell me, what do you think of him? 16. I can't tell you how happy I was. 17. Tell him to close the window.

Vocabularies

Genitive endings are given only for masculine and neuter nouns not forming the genitive in -(e)s. Plural endings are given for all nouns except feminines with plural ending -(e)n.

The definitions provided are for the contexts in this book.

ab-beißen to bite off
ab-schicken to send off
die Absicht intention
ähnlich similar
die Alpen Alps
das Altertum antiquity
Anderes different
sich ändern to change
anders differently
der Anfang, ⸗e beginning
an-fangen to begin, start
der Angestellte, -n, -n employee
an-kommen (ist) to arrive
an-nehmen to assume
an-sehen to regard
anstatt . . . zu instead of
an-stellen to employ
die Antike antiquity
sich an-ziehen to dress
der Anzug, ⸗e suit
die Apfelsine orange
ärgerlich angry
sich ärgern über to be angry at
arm poor
die Armut poverty
die Art kind, type
der Arzt, ⸗e physician
der Arztberuf medical profession
auf-bürden to burden with
aufeinander one another
die Aufgabe task, job
auf-hören to stop
auf-nehmen to receive; to absorb
der Aufsatz, ⸗e essay, article
auf-schreiben to write down
auf-stehen (ist) to get up
der Ausdruck, ⸗e expression
aus-drücken to express
aus-führen to take out
aus-geben to spend
ausgezeichnet excellent
aus-kommen (ist) to get along
das Ausland abroad
der Ausländer, - foreigner
aus-reißen to tear out
aus-sehen to look
außerdem besides
äußerst utmost
die Aussprache pronunciation
aus-üben to exert; to have
aus-wandern (ist) to emigrate
der Autounfall, ⸗e car accident

der Bach, ⸗e brook
das Bad, ⸗er bath

baden to bathe
der Bahnhof, ⸗e railroad station
der Bahnsteig, -e platform
bald soon
das Bandmaß, -e tape measure
bauen to build
der Bauer, -n farmer
der Baum, ⸗e tree
bayrisch Bavarian
der Beamte, -n, -n official
beantworten to answer
der Becher, - cup
bedeuten to mean
beeinflussen to influence
beenden to finish
befriedigen to satisfy
begeistert enthusiastic
behalten (behält), behielt, behalten to keep
behandeln to treat
behaupten to claim, assert
beherrschen to master
beide both, two
das Bein, -e leg
beißen, biß, gebissen to bite
bekannt known
bekommen, bekam, bekommen to get, receive
bemerken to notice
die Bemerkung remark
die Beobachtungsgabe power of observation
berechnen to calculate
bereisen to travel through
bereits already
berichten to report
der Beruf, -e profession
berühmt famous
beschäftigen to occupy
beschreiben, beschrieb, beschrieben to describe
besiegen to defeat
besitzen, besaß, besessen to possess
der Besitzer, - owner
besprechen (bespricht), besprach, besprochen to discuss
bestehen aus, bestand, bestanden to consist of
bestellen to order
besuchen to visit
betreffen (betrifft), betraf, betroffen to concern
die Bevölkerung population
die Bewegung movement
beweisen, bewies, bewiesen to prove
bewundern to admire
bezahlen to pay
die Bibliothek library

die **Biene** bee
bieten, bot, geboten to offer
das **Bild, -er** picture
bilden to form
billig cheap, inexpensive
bis until, up to
bißchen: ein bißchen a little (bit)
bitten, bat, gebeten to ask, request
blättern to turn over the pages
die **Blaubeere** blueberry
das **Blech** tin
das **Blei** lead
bleiben, blieb, ist geblieben to stay
der **Blitz, -e** lightning
die **Blume** flower
der **Blutdruck** blood pressure
bluten to bleed
der **Boden, =** ground, floor
die **Bonbons** (*pl.*) sweets, candy
böse angry, bad
brauchen to need
der **Breitengrad** degree of latitude
der **Brief, -e** letter
bringen, brachte, gebracht to bring, take
die **Brücke** bridge
brüllen to roar
der **Brunnen, -** well
die **Bühne** stage
der **Bundeskanzler, -** Chancellor
die **Burg** castle

der **Chemiker, -** chemist

das **Dach, =er** roof
damalig of that time
damals at that time
der **Dampfer, -** (steam)boat
darum therefore
dauern to last; take
davon-galoppieren (ist) to gallop away
die **Decke** cover
der **Deckel, -** lid
die **Delikatesse** delicacy
denken, dachte, gedacht to think
das **Denkmal, =er** monument
dennoch nevertheless
deutlich clearly
die **Deutschkenntnisse** (*pl.*) knowledge of German
der **Dichter, -** poet
dick thick, fat
der **Dieb, -e** thief
das **Ding, -e** thing
der **Dom, -e** cathedral
das **Dorf, =er** village
die **Drogerie** drugstore

dunkel dark
der **Durchbruch, =e** breakthrough
durchschnittlich average
der **Durst** thirst
das **Dutzend** dozen

edel noble
ehe before
das **Ei, -er** egg
eifrig eager
eigen own
ein-brechen to break in
der **Einbrecher, -** burglar
der **Einbruch, =e** burglary
einfach simple
der **Einfluß, =sse** influence
ein-führen to introduce; to import
der **Eingang, =e** entrance
einige some, a few
ein-laden to invite
einmal once
das **Einmaleins** multiplication table
einsam lonely
ein-sehen to understand, realize
die **Eintrittskarte** ticket
die **Einzelheit** detail
der **Einzelstaat, -en** individual state
die **Eisenbahn** railroad
die **Eltern** parents
empfehlen (empfiehlt), empfahl, empfohlen to recommend
endlich finally
entdecken to discover
die **Entdeckung** discovery
der **Entschluß, =sse** decision
(sich) entschuldigen to excuse (oneself)
das **Entwicklungsgesetz, -e** law of development
die **Erdbeere** strawberry
die **Erde** earth
die **Erfahrung** experience
sich erinnern to remember
erkennen, erkannte, erkannt to recognize
erklären to explain; to declare
die **Erklärung** explanation
erleben to experience
ermorden to murder
erobern to conquer
erreichen to reach
erscheinen, erschien, ist erschienen to appear, turn up
erschöpft exhausted
erschrecken to frighten, startle
erst first; not until
erwähnen to mention
erwarten to expect

das **Erwarten** expectation
erzählen to tell
das **Essen** food; dinner
etwa perhaps, approximately
etwas something, some; **so etwas** something like that
das **Experiment, -e** experiment

die **Fabrik** factory
das **Fach, ‡er** subject
der **Fähnrich, -e** ensign
die **Fahrkarte** ticket
die **Fahrt** trip
der **Fall, ‡e** case
der **Fang** catch
die **Farbe** color
fast almost
die **Faust, ‡e** fist
die **Feder** pen
der **Fehler, -** mistake, error
feiern to celebrate
der **Feiertag, -e** holiday
der **Feind, -e** enemy
feindlich hostile
das **Feld, -er** field
das **Feldlazarett, -e** field hospital
der **Felsen, -** rock
das **Fenster, -** window
die **Ferien** (*pl.*) vacation
das **Fernsehen** television
fest firm, tight
das **Feuer** fire; light
finden, fand, gefunden to find; **sich finden** to be found
die **Firma, Firmen** firm
die **Fläche** surface
das **Fleisch** meat
die **Fleischerei** meat market
die **Fliege** fly
fliegen, flog, ist geflogen to fly
der **Flieger, -** flyer
der **Flüchtling, -e** refugee
der **Flug, ‡e** flight
das **Flugzeug, -e** airplane
der **Fluß, ‡sse** river
die **Folge** consequence
folgen (ist) to follow
der **Forscher, -** research worker
fort-fahren (ist) to leave
der **Fortschritt, -e** progress
fort-setzen to continue
die **Frage** question
fragen to ask
(das) **Frankreich** France
der **Franzose, -n, -n** Frenchman
französisch French

die **Frau** woman; wife
die **Freiheit** freedom, liberty
der **Fremdling, -e** stranger
sich freuen to be glad; **sich freuen auf** to look forward to
der **Friede(n)** peace
der **Friseur, -e** barber, hairdresser
froh glad, gay
die **Frucht, ‡e** fruit
fruchtlos fruitless
früh early
der **Frühling** spring
das **Frühstück** breakfast
fühlen to feel
führen to lead
der **Fund** find
die **Fußballmannschaft** football team

ganz entire, whole
gar: gar nicht not at all
der **Gasherd, -e** gas range
der **Gast, ‡e** guest
das **Gebäude, -** building
geben (gibt), gab, gegeben to give; **es gibt** there is, are
das **Gebiet, -e** field
das **Gebirge, -** mountains
gebraten (*p.p.*) roasted
gebrauchen to use
der **Gebrauchtwagen, -** used car
der **Gedanke, -ns, -n** thought
die **Gefahr** danger
gefallen (gefällt), gefiel, gefallen to like
der **Gefangene, -n, -n** prisoner
die **Gegend** region, neighborhood
die **Gegenwart** present
der **Gegner, -** opponent
gehen, ging, ist gegangen to go; **es geht ihm schlecht** he is not well
gehorchen to obey
gehören to belong
der **Geist** spirit
gekocht (*p.p.*) boiled
das **Geld** money
die **Gelegenheit** occasion, opportunity
der **Gelehrte, -n, -n** scholar
gelingen, gelang, ist gelungen to succeed
genau exactly, accurately, very well, in detail
das **Genie, -s** genius
genug enough
genügen to be sufficient; **genügend** sufficiently
das **Gepäck** luggage
gering little

gern; ich habe gern, lieber, am liebsten I like, prefer, like best

der **Gesamteindruck** ⸗e general impression

das **Geschäft, -e** store, business
geschäftlich business (*adj.*)

der **Geschäftsfreund, -e** business friend

der **Geschäftsmann, . . . leute** businessman
geschehen (geschieht), geschah, ist ge- schehen to happen

das **Geschenkpaket, -e** gift package

die **Geschichte** history
geschickt skilled

das **Geschirr** dishes

der **Geschmack** taste

die **Geschwister** sisters and brothers

die **Gesellschaft** company

das **Gesetz, -e** law

das **Gesicht, -er** face

das **Gespräch, -e** conversation

die **Gestalt** form, figure
gestern yesterday

die **Gesundheit** health

die **Gesundheitsregel** rule of health
geteilt (*p.p.*) divided

die **Gewalt** power
gewiß surely

das **Gewitter, -** thunderstorm
sich gewöhnen an to become accustomed to
gießen, goß, gegossen to pour
giftig poisonous

der **Glanz** brightness
glänzen to glitter

die **Glaskugel** glass bead
glauben to believe
gleich same

der **Gletscher, -** glacier
glücklich happy

die **Grammatik** grammar

die **Grenze** border

(das) **Griechenland** Greece

die **Großkatze** big cat

die **Großstadt,** ⸗e (large) city, metropolis

der **Grund,** ⸗e reason, cause
gültig valid
günstig favorable
gutgemeint well-meant
gutherzig good-hearted

der **Hafen,** ⸗ harbor

der **Hagel** hail

der **Hahn,** ⸗e rooster

die **Halbwahrheit** half-truth

der **Halt** hold, footing
halten (hält), hielt, gehalten to hold, keep; to stop
handeln to act; **handeln von** to deal with

der **Handschuh, -e** glove
häßlich ugly

die **Hauptattraktion** main attraction

die **Hauptrolle** leading role
häuslich domestic

das **Heer, -e** army

die **Heimat** home(land)
heiraten to marry
heißen, hieß, geheißen to be called; to mean

der **Held, -en, -en** hero
helfen (hilft), half, geholfen to help
hell clear

das **Hemd, -en** shirt
heraus-fordern to challenge

das **Herrengeschäft, -e** men's store
herrlich delightful, glorious, wonderful
herrschend dominating

der **Herrscher, -** ruler, master

die **Hilfe** help

der **Himmel** sky, heaven
sich hin-setzen to sit down
hinter- rear

die **Hitze** heat
hochgebildet highly educated

die **Hochzeit** wedding

der **Hof,** ⸗e courtyard
hoffentlich I hope

die **höhere Schule** secondary school
holen to fetch, get, take

das **Holz** wood

der **Hornstoß,** ⸗e thrust of the horns

der **Hosenträger, -** suspenders

der **Hoteldiener, -** bellboy
hübsch pretty
hügelig hilly

das **Huhn,** ⸗er chicken

der **Hund, -e** dog

der **Husten** cough

irgend jemand anybody

der **Jäger, -** hunter
jagen to hunt
jahrelang for years

das **Jahrhundert, -e** century
je ever

das **Jugendwerk, -e** first (early) work

der **Junge, -n, -n** boy

kahl bald
kämpfen to fight

die **Kartoffel** potato

der **Kartoffelsalat** potato salad

der **Käse** cheese

der **Kassierer, -** cashier, teller

die **Katze** cat
kaufen to buy
der **Kaufmann, . . . leute** businessman
kaum hardly
der **Kellner, -** waiter
kennen, kannte, gekannt to know
das **Kino, -s** movies; movie theater
die **Kirche** church
klagen to complain
klar clear
das **Klavier, -e** piano
das **Kleid, -er** dress; (*pl.*) clothing
klettern (ist) to climb
klingen, klang, geklungen to sound
klopfen to knock
klug smart, clever
der **Koffer, -** suitcase
der **Kommilitone, -n, -n** fellow student
komponieren to compose
die **Konditorei** pastry shop, café
der **König, -e** king
der **Konkurrent, -en, -en** competitor
der **Konzertbesucher, -** concert goer
der **Kopf, -e** head
die **Kopfschmerzen** (*pl.*) headache
der **Körper, -** body
die **Kosten** (*pl.*) cost, charges; **auf Kosten**
at the expense
die **Kraft, -e** strength
kräftig strong
krank ill
die **Krankheit** illness
der **Kreis, -e** circle
kriechen, kroch, ist gekrochen to crawl
der **Krieg, -e** war
kriegen to get
der **Kriegsgefangene, -n, -n** prisoner of war
das **Kriegsschiff, -e** warship
der **Kuchen** cake
das **Küchenmesser, -** kitchen knife
die **Kugel** bullet
der **Kühlschrank, -e** refrigerator
die **Kultur** culture
kümmern to concern; **sich kümmern um**
to care about
der **Kunde, -n, -n** customer
die **Kunst, -e** art
der **Künstler, -** artist
kurz short
die **Küste** coast

der **Laden, -** store
das **Ladenschild, -er** (store)sign
die **Lage** location
das **Lager, -** camp
das **Landhaus, -er** country home

die **Landschaft** countryside
langsam slow
der **Lärm** noise
laufen (läuft), lief, ist gelaufen to run
leicht light; easy
leider unfortunately
der **Leser, -** reader
die **Leute** (*pl.*) people
lieben to love
das **Lied, -er** song
liegen, lag, gelegen to lie
loben to praise
lösen to solve
die **Lösung** solution
der **Löwe, -n, -n** lion
die **Luft** air
die **Luftpost** airmail
lügen, log, gelogen to (tell a) lie
lustig amusing, funny

das **Mal, -e** time
manchmal sometimes
die **Mannschaft** team
der **Mantel, -** coat
das **Märchen, -** fairy tale
die **Masse** the masses, people
die **Mauer** wall
das **Meer, -e** ocean
der **Mensch, -en, -en** man, person
menschlich human
merken to notice
das **Messer, -** knife
die **Metallkugel** metal ball
der **Mitarbeiter, -** fellow worker
miteinander with one another
mit-gehen (ist) to go along
die **Mittel** (*pl.*) means, resources
das **Mittelalter** Middle Ages
mittelalterlich medieval
das **Mittelmeer** Mediterranean
der **Mittelpunkt** center
die **Mitternacht** midnight
möglich possible
das **Mondlicht** moonlight
der **Monat, -e** month
das **Monatsgehalt, -er** monthly salary
der **Mord, -e** murder
das **Motorrad, -er** motorcycle
müde tired

der **Nachbar, -n** neighbor
die **Nachbarschaft** neighborhood
der **Nachbartisch, -e** next table
die **Nachricht** news
die **Nachwelt** posterity
der **Nagel, -** nail

die **Nähe** vicinity
die **Nase** nose
der **Nasenring, -e** nose ring
der **Nebel, -** fog
der **Neffe, -n, -n** nephew
  nehmen (nimmt), nahm, genommen to
    take
  nett nice
das **Netz, -e** net
  neugeboren newborn
  nichts nothing
  nie never
  niemand nobody
  noch still
  nötig necessary; **nötig haben** to need
die **Notwendigkeit** necessity
die **Null** zero

  ob if, whether
  oben above
  obgleich although
  operieren to operate
der **Ozeandampfer, -** transatlantic steamer

  paar: ein paar a few
das **Päckchen, -** package
das **Papier, -e** paper
die **Papierhandlung** stationery store
der **Papst, ⸗e** Pope
der **Paß, ⸗sse** passport
  passieren, (ist) to happen
der **Pelzmantel, ⸗** fur coat
  pfeifen, pfiff, gepfiffen to whistle
das **Pferd, -e** horse; **zu Pferde** on horseback
das **Pferdehaar, -e** horsehair
die **Pflicht** duty
  pflücken to pick
  plagen to plague
  plötzlich suddenly
(das) **Polen** Poland
  preisen, pries, gepriesen to praise
der **Privateingang, ⸗e** private entrance
  prüfen to test
die **Prüfung** examination
die **Puppe** doll

  qualvoll painful

die **Rakete** rocket
  rammen to ram, drive
  rasen, (ist) to rush
  rastlos restless
der **Rat, ⸗e** advice
  raten (rät), riet, geraten to advise
  rauchen to smoke
  rechnen zu to include in

die **Rechnung** bill
  recht right; **recht haben** to be right
das **Recht, -e** right
die **Rede** speech
der **Regen** rain
  regnen to rain
das **Reich, -e** empire
  reichen to hand
die **Reihe** row; **an der Reihe sein** or **an die**
    Reihe kommen to be one's turn
die **Reise** trip
der **Reiseführer, -** guide(book)
  reißen, riß, gerissen to tear
  reiten, ritt, ist geritten to ride (on horse-
    back)
die **Reklame** advertisement
das **Rennen** race
das **Rennpferd, -e** racehorse
die **Reparatur** repair
  retten to save
  richtig correct; real
der **Riese, -n, -n** giant
der **Riesenbär, -en** giant bear
  riesig huge
der **Riß, ⸗sse** tear, split
der **Roman, -e** novel
  rufen, rief, gerufen to call
  ruhen to rest
  ruhig quiet
der **Ruhm** fame

die **Sache** thing
die **Sahne** cream
die **Salbe** salve
die **Sammlung** collection
der **Satz, ⸗e** sentence
der **Säugling, -e** baby
die **Schaffenskraft** creative power
  scharf sharp; harsh
der **Schatten, -** shadow
der **Schauspieler, -** actor
  schenken to give (as a present), present
  schicken to send
das **Schicksal** fate
der **Schimmel, -** white horse
der **Schinken** ham
die **Schlacht** battle
  schlagen (schlägt), schlug, geschlagen to
    hit, beat
die **Schlange** snake
  schlecht bad
der **Schlepper, -** tugboat
  schließlich finally, at last
das **Schloß, ⸗sser** castle
der **Schluß** end, conclusion
  schmeicheln to flatter

der **Schmerz, -en** pain
  schmerzend aching
  schmerzhaft painful
  schmutzig dirty
  schneiden, schnitt, geschnitten to cut
der **Schneider, -** tailor
  schnell fast, quick
die **Schnelligkeit** quickness, speed
  schön beautiful
der **Schreck** fright
der **Schrei, -e** cry, scream
die **Schreibmaschine** typewriter
der **Schreibtisch, -e** writing desk
  schreien, schrie, geschrieen to scream
der **Schriftsteller, -** writer, author
der **Schritt, -e** step
die **Schulden** (*pl.*) debts
der **Schüler, -** pupil
die **Schulter** shoulder
  schütteln to shake
der **Schutz** protection
  schützen to protect
der **Schützengraben, =** trench
der **Schutzmann, . . . leute** policeman
  schwach weak; low
das **Schwarzbrot, -e** rye bread
der **Schwarzwald** Black Forest
  schweben to hover
das **Schweigen** silence
der **Schweißtropfen, -** drop of perspiration
die **Schweiz** Switzerland
  schwer heavy; difficult, hard
das **Schwert, -er** sword
die **Schwierigkeit** difficulty, problem
der **See, -n** lake
die **See** sea, ocean
das **Seebad, =er** seaside resort
die **Seemannsstiefel** (*pl.*) sailor's boots
das **Segelboot, -e** sailboat
die **Sehenswürdigkeiten** (*pl.*) sights
die **Sehnsucht** longing
die **Seite** page
  selbst himself; even
  setzen to put, place
  seufzen to sigh
  sicher certain, sure
  sichtbar visible
der **Sieg, -e** victory
  siegen to win
die **Sitte** custom
  sitzen, saß, gesessen to sit
der **Smaragd, -e** emerald
  sofort immediately
  sogar even
  sogenannt so-called
der **Soldat, -en, -en** soldier

die **Sommerferien** (*pl.*) summer vacation
die **Sorge** worry
  sorgen to care (for)
  spät late
  spazieren-gehen to go for a walk
die **Speisekarte** menu
der **Speisesaal, . . . säle** dining room
das **Spezialgebiet, -e** special field of interest
  spielen to play
die **Sprache** language
das **Sprichwort, =er** proverb
  spülen: das Geschirr spülen to wash the dishes
die **Spur** trace, track, remains
  spüren to feel
der **Staat, -en** state
die **Stadt, =e** city
das **Stadtviertel, -** part of town
das **Stadtzentrum** center of the city
  stammen aus to date from; to come from
die **Stärke** strength
  stehen, stand, gestanden to stand; to be (written)
  steigen, stieg, ist gestiegen to climb, rise; to board
die **Stelle** spot, place; passage
  stellen to place, put
die **Stellung** position
die **Steuern** (*pl.*) taxes
der **Stich, -e** bite
der **Stier, -e** bull
der **Stierkämpfer, -** bullfighter
  stolpern (ist) to trip
  stolz proud
das **Storchnest, -er** stork nest
  stören to disturb
der **Stoß, =e** thrust
der **Strahl, -en** ray
die **Strapaze** hardship
die **Straße** street
die **Straßenbahn** streetcar
die **Strecke** distance
der **Streit, -e** quarrel, argument
der **Streifen, -** stripe, streak
  streng strict
die **Strömung** current
das **Stück, -e** piece
das **Studium, Studien** study
die **Stunde** hour
  stundenlang for hours
der **Sturz** fall, plunge
  stürzen (ist) to fall, plunge
  suchen to seek, look for
die **Sünde** sin
  sündig sinful
die **Süßigkeiten** sweets

das **Tal**, ⸗er valley
die **Tapferkeit** bravery
die **Tasche** pocket
die **Tasse** cup
die **Tat** deed
die **Tatsache** fact
    taub deaf
die **Technik** technology
der **Teelöffel**, - teaspoon
der **Teil**, -e part
    teuer expensive
das **Theaterstück**, -e play
das **Thema, Themen** subject, topic
    tief deep
die **Tiefe** depth, abyss
das **Tier**, -e animal
der **Tod** death
    tödlich fatal, mortal
das **Tor**, -e gate
die **Torheit** foolishness
    tot dead
    töten to kill
    tragen (trägt), trug, getragen to carry;
      to wear
die **Träne** tear
    trauen to trust
der **Traum**, ⸗e dream
der **Träumer**, - dreamer
    traurig sad, gloomy
    treffen (trifft), traf, getroffen to hit; to
      meet
    treten (tritt), trat, ist getreten to step
    treu faithful
das **Trinkgeld**, -er tip
    trotz in spite of
die **Tulpe** tulip
    tun, tat, getan to do
der **Turm**, ⸗e tower

    üben to practice
    übersehen (übersieht), übersah, übersehen
      to overlook
    übersetzen to translate
    überzeugen to convince
    übrig remaining
die **Übung** practice
das **Ufer**, - shore
    ungesund unhealthy
    ungewöhnlich unusual
    unmöglich impossible
    unsterblich immortal
der **Untergang** fall
    unternehmen (unternimmt), unternahm,
      unternommen to undertake
das **Unterseeboot**, -e submarine
    untersuchen to examine, investigate

die **Untersuchung** investigation, research
die **Untertasse** saucer
die **Ursache** cause
das **Urteil**, -e judgment
der **Urwald**, ⸗er jungle

das **Veilchen**, - violet
die **Veränderung** change
die **Verantwortung** responsibility
    verdächtig suspicious
    verdienen to earn
    verehren to respect, revere
die **Verfügung: zur Verfügung stehen** to be
      at the disposal
die **Vergangenheit** past
    vergehen, verging, ist vergangen to pass
    vergessen (vergißt), vergaß, vergessen to
      forget
    vergleichen, verglich, verglichen to com-
      pare
die **Verhältnisse** (*pl.*) circumstances
    verheiratet (*p.p.*) married
    verkaufen to sell
der **Verkehr** traffic
    verlangen to demand
    verlassen (verläßt), verließ, verlassen to
      leave
    verleben to spend
der **Verlust**, -e loss
    vernünftig reasonable
    veröffentlichen to publish
    verschieden different
    verschwinden, verschwand, ist verschwun-
      den to disappear
das **Versprechen**, - promise
das **Verständnis** understanding
    verstehen, verstand, verstanden to under-
      stand
der **Versuch**, -e experiment
der **Verwandte**, -n, -n relative
    verwunden to wound
    verwundert surprised
der **Verwundete**, -n, -n wounded soldier
    verzeihen, verzieh, verziehen to forgive
der **Vetter**, -n cousin
    vielleicht perhaps
das **Viertel** quarter
der **Viertelliter**, - quarter liter
der **Vogel**, ⸗ bird
das **Volksfest**, -e national festival
sich **vor-bereiten** to prepare oneself
    vorderste foremost, first
    vor-gehen to be fast
    vorig previous, last
    vor-lesen to read aloud
die **Vorlesung** lecture

die **Vorsicht** caution
vor-spielen to play something to a person
sich (acc.) **vor-stellen** to introduce oneself;
  sich (dat.) **vor-stellen** to imagine
der **Vortrag, ≃e** lecture
vorwiegend predominantly

wachsen (wächst), wuchs, ist gewachsen
  to grow
der **Wagen, -** car
während while
die **Wahrheit** truth
wahrscheinlich probably
der **Wald, ≃er** forest
die **Wand, ≃e** wall
die **Wanderung** hike
der **Wandschrank, ≃e** closet
die **Wange** cheek
warnen to warn
die **Wasserschlange** water snake
weder ... noch neither ... nor
weg-ziehen to pull away
Weihnachten Christmas
der **Weihnachtsbaum, ≃e** Christmas tree
weiter further, farther
weiter-kämpfen to fight on
weltberühmt world famous
der **Weltkrieg, -e** World War
die **Weltliteratur** world literature
wenig little; not very; **weniger** less
wenigstens at least
werfen (wirft), warf, geworfen to throw,
  cast
der **Wert, -e** value
Wertvolles: nichts Wertvolles nothing
  of value
westfälisch Westphalian
das **Wetter** weather
wichtig important
wider against, contrary to
der **Widerstand** resistance
sich widmen to devote oneself
wiederholen to repeat

wirken to take effect
wirklich really, actually
die **Wirkung** effect
die **Wirtin, -nen** landlady
wissen (weiß), wußte, gewußt to know
die **Wissenschaft** science
der **Wissenschaftler, -** scientist
witzig witty; ingenious
die **Woche** week
woher from what place; how
wohnen to live
die **Wohnung** apartment
die **Wolke** cloud
wolkenlos cloudless
womit with which, through which
der **Wunsch, ≃e** wish
wünschen to wish, desire
die **Wut** rage

zahlen to pay
die **Zauberkraft** magic power
zeigen to show
der **Zeitgenosse, -n, -n** contemporary
die **Zeitschrift** periodical
die **Zeitung** newspaper
zerstören to destroy
der **Zettel, -** piece of paper
das **Ziel, -e** goal, aim
zitieren to quote
das **Zimmer, -** room
zittern to tremble
die **Zivilbevölkerung** (civilian) population
zuerst at first
der **Zufall, ≃e** chance, accident
zufällig accidentally, by chance
der **Zug, ≃e** train
die **Zukunft** future
zu-machen to close
die **Zunge** tongue
zusammen-brechen (ist) to collapse
der **Zuschauer, -** spectator
zwecklos useless
zweifelhaft doubtful

absent abwesend
action die Handlung
address die Adresse
advantage der Vorteil, -e
advice der Rat
ago vor
air die Luft
airplane das Flugzeug, -e
all ganz; (*pl.*) alle
already schon
always immer
American amerikanisch; **the American** der
  Amerikaner,
ancient alt
angry böse
another noch ein
answer die Antwort
answer antworten, beantworten
anybody jemand
anymore: **not anymore** nicht mehr
anything (irgend) etwas; **not anything** nichts
appear erscheinen, erschien, ist erschienen
apple der Apfel, =
appointment die Verabredung
around um . . . herum
arrive an-kommen (ist)
article der Artikel, -
as als; wie
ask fragen
at in, auf, bei; **not at all** gar nicht
attend besuchen
aunt die Tante

baby das Baby, -s; das kleine Kind, -er
back zurück
bad schlecht
bag die Handtasche
bank die Bank
bar das Stück, -e
barefoot barfuß
beat schlagen (schlägt), schlug, geschlagen
beautiful schön
because weil; **because of** wegen
bed das Bett, -en
before vor; bevor; **never before** noch nie
begin an-fangen
beginning der Anfang, =e
believe glauben
beyond über . . . hinaus
Bible die Bibel
big groß
bill die Rechnung
birthday party die Geburtstagsfeier
blow der Schlag, =e
blue blau
blush erröten (ist)

book das Buch, =er
bookshelf das Bücherbrett, -er
boring langweilig
box office die Theaterkasse
boy der Junge, -n, -n
bread das Brot, -e
break brechen (bricht), brach, gebrochen
breathe atmen
bridge die Brücke
briefcase die Aktentasche
bring along mit-bringen
brother der Bruder, =
burn verbrennen, verbrannte, verbrannt
bus der Autobus, . . . busse
butcher der Fleischer, -
butter die Butter
buttonhole das Knopfloch, =er
buy kaufen

cabin die Kabine
café das Café, -s
cake der Kuchen, -
call up an-rufen
candle die Kerze
captain der Kapitän, -e
car der Wagen, -
carry tragen (trägt), trug, getragen
catalogue der Katalog, -e
cathedral der Dom, -e
century das Jahrhundert, -e; **for centuries**
  jahrhundertelang
chair der Stuhl, =e
character der Charakter
cheap billig
check prüfen, kontrollieren
cheese der Käse
child das Kind, -er
chlorine das Chlor
chocolate die Schokolade
choose wählen
Christmas Weihnachten
church die Kirche
cigar die Zigarre
cigarette die Zigarette
city die Stadt, =e
class die Klasse; die Stunde
clean up auf-räumen
clear klar
close schließen, schloß, geschlossen; zu-
  machen
club der Klub, -s
coat der Mantel, =
coffee der Kaffee
cold kalt
collection die Sammlung
come kommen, kam, ist gekommen; **come**

along mit-kommen; **come back** wieder-
kommen
concert das Konzert, -e
conductor der Schaffner, -
connection die Verbindung
convince überzeugen
cook kochen
corner die Ecke
corridor der Gang, ⸗e
country das Land, ⸗er; **in the country** auf
dem Land
cover die Bettdecke
crazy verrückt
critic der Rezensent, -en, -en
criticize kritisieren
cup die Tasse, der Becher, -

dance tanzen
dark dunkel
daughter die Tochter, ⸗
day der Tag, -e
decision die Entscheidung
deep tief
deny leugnen
deserve verdienen
diamond der Diamant, -en, -en
dinner das Abendessen
direct direkt
direction die Richtung
director der Direktor, -en
discover entdecken
discuss besprechen (bespricht), besprach, besprochen
discussion die Diskussion
dish die Schüssel; **to wash the dishes** das
Geschirr spülen
dissertation die Dissertation
disturb stören
do tun, tat, getan
door die Tür
dot der Punkt, -e
dress das Kleid, -er
drive (im Wagen) fahren (fährt), fuhr, ist gefahren
duty die Pflicht

each jeder; **each other** einander
ear das Ohr, -en
early früh
easy leicht
eat essen (ißt), aß, gegessen
egg das Ei, -er
empty leer
end das Ende
enough genug
error der Fehler, -
escape entkommen, entkam, ist entkommen

Europe (das) Europa
even though obgleich
evening der Abend, -e
every jeder; **everything** alles
everywhere überall
exact genau
examination die Prüfung
experience die Erfahrung; das Erlebnis, -se
experiment das Experiment, -e
explain erklären
express oneself sich aus-drücken
eye das Auge, -n

face das Gesicht, -er
fall asleep ein-schlafen (ist)
family die Familie
fanatical fanatisch
father der Vater, ⸗
few: a few einige, ein paar; wenige
film der Film, -e
finally endlich
find finden, fand, gefunden
finger der Finger, -
finish beenden; **to have finished** fertig sein
firm fest
first erst-
fish der Fisch, -e
flower die Blume
fly fliegen, flog, ist geflogen
follow folgen (ist)
foot der Fuß, ⸗e
football der Fußball, ⸗e
forever ewig
forget vergessen (vergißt), vergaß, vergessen
French (das) Französisch
friend der Freund, -e
friendship die Freundschaft
frost der Frost

game das Spiel, -e
garage die Garage
gentleman der Herr, -en, -en
German deutsch; (das) Deutsch
Germany (das) Deutschland
get (become) werden (wird), wurde, ist geworden; **to get along with** aus-kommen
mit; **to get up** auf-stehen
girl das Mädchen, -
give geben (gibt), gab, gegeben
glad froh
glass das Glas, ⸗er
go gehen, ging, ist gegangen; fahren (fährt),
fuhr, ist gefahren; **to go out** aus-gehen
God (der) Gott
government die Regierung
grandmother die Grossmutter, ⸗

grass das Gras
ground der Boden

hair das Haar, -e
ham der Schinken, -
hand die Hand, ⸗e
handbag die Handtasche
happen geschehen (geschieht), geschah, ist geschehen; passieren (ist)
happy glücklich
hard hart; schwer; **something hard** etwas Hartes
hardly kaum
hat der Hut, ⸗e
hear hören
heart das Herz, -ens, -en
help helfen (hilft), half, geholfen
hold halten (hält), hielt, gehalten
home nach Hause; **(at) home** zu Hause
homework die Schulaufgaben (*pl.*)
hope hoffen
hospital das Krankenhaus, ⸗er
hotel das Hotel, -s
hotel room das Hotelzimmer, -
hour die Stunde; **for hours** stundenlang
house das Haus, ⸗er
how wie
hungry hungrig; **to be hungry** Hunger haben
husband der Mann, ⸗er

if ob
ill krank
illustrate illustrieren
important wichtig
impossible unmöglich
information die Information, die Auskunft
interest interessieren; **to be interested in** sich interessieren für
interesting interessant
invite ein-laden

joke der Witz, -e
just eben

key der Schlüssel, -
kind: **what kind of** was für ein
kitchen die Küche
kitchen table der Küchentisch, -e
knee das Knie, -
knife das Messer, -
know wissen (weiß), wußte, gewußt; kennen, kannte, gekannt
known bekannt

ladder die Leiter
lamp die Lampe

landlady die Wirtin, -nen
language die Sprache
large groß
last letzt-; **last night** gestern abend; **at last** endlich
late spät; **to be late** sich verspäten
lead führen
learn lernen
leave lassen (läßt), ließ, gelassen; verlassen (verläßt), verließ, verlassen; fort-gehen (ist); **leave for** ab-reisen nach (ist)
lecture die Vorlesung, der Vortrag, ⸗e
lesson die Aufgabe
let lie liegen lassen
letter der Brief, -e; der Buchstabe, -ns, -n
library die Bibliothek
lie die Lüge
(tell a) lie lügen, log, gelogen
lieutenant der Leutnant, -s
life das Leben
like mögen (mag), mochte, gemocht; gefallen (gefällt), gefiel, gefallen; **Would you like?** Möchten Sie?
limited beschränkt
literature die Literatur
little klein; wenig; **a little** etwas
live leben, wohnen
long lang; **no longer** nicht mehr
look aus-sehen; **to look at** an-sehen
lose verlieren, verlor, verloren
loss der Verlust, -e
love lieben
lunch das Mittagessen

Magic Mountain der Zauberberg
mail die Post
mailbox der Briefkasten, ⸗
man der Mann, ⸗er; der Mensch, -en, -en
many viele
map die Karte
marketplace der Marktplatz, ⸗e
marry heiraten
mathematics die Mathematik
mean meinen; bedeuten
meat das Fleisch
mechanic der Mechaniker, -
medicine die Medizin
meet kennen-lernen
meeting die Versammlung
member das Mitglied, -er
memories die Erinnerungen
milk die Milch
minute die Minute
miserly geizig
mistake der Fehler, -
modern modern

moisture   die Feuchtigkeit
moment   der Moment, -e
money   das Geld
month   der Monat, -e; **for months**   monate-
lang
morning   der Morgen; **this morning**   heute
früh
most   die meisten
mother   die Mutter, =
motorcycle   das Motorrad, =er
motto   das Motto, -s
mouth   der Mund
movie(s)   das Kino, -s
moving picture   der Film, -e
much   viel
museum   das Museum, Museen
music   die Musik

name   der Name(n), -ns, -n
need   brauchen
neighbor   der Nachbar, -n
neither . . . nor   weder . . . noch
never   nie
new   neu
news   die Nachricht
next   nächst-; nebenan
night   die Nacht, =e; **last night**   gestern abend
noise   der Lärm
nothing   nichts
novel   der Roman, -e
now   jetzt

o'clock   Uhr
office   das Büro, -s
official   der Beamte, -n, -n; ein Beamter
onion   die Zwiebel
only   nur
open   öffnen
opera   die Oper
opinion   die Meinung
order   die Ordnung
order   bestellen
other   ander-
owner   der Besitzer, -

page   die Seite
pain   der Schmerz, -en
paint   an-streichen
paper   das Papier, -e
parents   die Eltern
parking lot   der Parkplatz, =e
part   der Teil, -e
participant   der Teilnehmer, -
party   die Gesellschaft
passenger   der Passagier, -e
passport   der Paß, =sse

pay   bezahlen
pencil   der Bleistift, -e
penny   der Pfennig, -e
people   die Leute (*pl.*)
performance   die Aufführung
permission   die Erlaubnis
person   die Person
philosopher   der Philosoph, -en, -en
philosophy   die Philosophie
piano   das Klavier, -e
picture   das Bild, -er; der Film, -e
piece   das Stück, -e
pipe   die Röhre
place   der Platz, =e
plan   der Plan, =e
play   das Stück, -e, das Theaterstück, -e
play   spielen
plenty of   viel
pocket   die Tasche
pocketbook   die Brieftasche
poem   das Gedicht, -e
political   politisch
poor   arm
possible   möglich
post office   das Postamt, =er
pound   das Pfund; **by the pound**   pfund**weise**
praise   loben
present   das Geschenk, -e
present   anwesend
price   der Preis, -e
program   das Programm, -e
pulse   der Puls
punch   lochen
purpose   der Zweck, -e

question   die Frage
quick   schnell
quiet   ruhig

race   das Rennen, -
rain   der Regen
rain   regnen
raise   die Gehaltserhöhung
read   lesen (liest), las, gelesen
ready   bereit, fertig
really   wirklich
receive   erhalten (erhält), erhielt, erhalten
record   der Rekord, -e
refrigerator   der Kühlschrank, =e
reliable   zuverlässig
remedy   das Mittel, -
remind of   erinnern an
repair   reparieren
responsible   verantwortlich
responsibility   die Verantwortung
restaurant   das Restaurant, -s

return   zurück-kehren (ist)
ribbon   das Band, ⸗er
rich   reich
right   richtig
ring   der Ring, -e
road   die Straße
room   das Zimmer, ⸗; **room number**   die Zimmernummer
rose   die Rose
rule   die Regel
Russian   (das) Russisch

sad   traurig
salad   der Salat, -e
salary   das Gehalt, ⸗er
salesman   der Verkäufer, -
salt   das Salz
same: the same   derselbe
Saturday   Sonnabend, Samstag
sauce   die Tunke
say   sagen
school   die Schule
schoolmate   der Schulkamerad, -en, -en
second   zweit-
secure   sorglos
see   sehen (sieht), sah, gesehen
selection   die Auswahl
sell   verkaufen
several   mehrere
shoe   der Schuh, -e
shore   das Ufer, -
shoulder   die Schulter
show   zeigen
sick   krank
sing   singen, sang, gesungen
sister   die Schwester
sit down   sich hin-setzen
skating   (das) Schlittschuhlaufen
skiing   (das) Schilaufen
sleep   schlafen (schläft), schlief, geschlafen
slender   schlank
slight   gering
small   klein
smile   lächeln
smoke   rauchen
soap   die Seife
soldier   der Soldat, -en, -en
somebody   jemand
someone   jemand
something   etwas
song   das Lied, -er
soon   bald
soup   die Suppe
sour   sauer
speak   sprechen (spricht), sprach, gesprochen
spring   der Frühling

stage   die Bühne
start   beginnen, begann, begonnen
station   der Bahnhof, ⸗e; die Bahnhofshalle
stay   bleiben, blieb, ist geblieben
still   noch
stone   der Stein, -e
store   der Laden, ⸗; das Geschäft, -e
story   die Geschichte
stranger   der Fremde, -n, -n; ein Fremder
street   die Straße
student   der Student, -en, -en
subway   die Untergrundbahn
such   solch; (*pl.*) solche
suit   der Anzug, ⸗e
summer   der Sommer, ⸗; **all summer**   den ganzen Sommer
sweet   süss
swim   schwimmen, schwamm, ist geschwommen

table   der Tisch, -e
table tennis   das Tischtennis
take   nehmen (nimmt), nahm, genommen; **take over**   übernehmen
talk   sprechen (spricht), sprach, gesprochen; reden
tall   groß
taxi   das Taxi, die Taxe
tea   der Tee
telephone   das Telephon, -e
telephone number   die Telephonnummer
tell   sagen; erzählen
test   die Prüfung
than   als
theater   das Theater, -
there   dort, dorthin
thick   dick
thing   das Ding, -e; **the right thing**   das Richtige; **not a thing**   nichts
think   denken, dachte, gedacht; **to think of**   halten von
this   dieser
ticket   die Eintrittskarte, die Fahrkarte
time   die Zeit; **another time**   ein anderes Mal; **for a long time**   lange; **on time**   pünktlich
tired   müde
title   der Titel, -
today   heute
tomorrow   morgen
tonight   heute abend
too   auch; zu
tower   der Turm, ⸗e
town   die Stadt, ⸗e
trade   das Handwerk, -e
train   der Zug, ⸗e
translation   die Übersetzung

travel reisen (ist)
trip die Reise
tropical tropisch
true wahr
trunk der Koffer, -
truth die Wahrheit
try versuchen
turning point der Wendepunkt

umbrella der Regenschirm, -e
understand verstehen, verstand, verstanden
unhappy unglücklich
university die Universität
unsure unsicher
use gebrauchen; used car der Gebrauchtwagen, -

vacation die Ferien (*pl.*)
vase die Vase
vending machine der Automat, -en, -en
vicinity die Nähe; in the vicinity nahe bei
visit besuchen
voice die Stimme

wait warten
wake up auf-wachen (ist)
walk der Spaziergang, ⹀e; to take a walk
einen Spaziergang machen
walk gehen, ging, ist gegangen
wall die Wand, ⹀e; die Mauer
war der Krieg, -e
wash waschen (wäscht), wusch, gewaschen;
to wash the dishes das Geschirr spülen

water das Wasser; waters das Gewässer
way der Weg, -e
weak schwach
Wednesday der Mittwoch
week die Woche
well gut; wohl
Westphalian westfälisch
wet naß
when wann; wenn, als
where wo
while während, solange
who wer
why warum
widow die Witwe
wife die Frau
win gewinnen, gewann, gewonnen
window das Fenster, -
wine der Wein, -e
winter der Winter, -
without ohne; without *plus -ing form* ohne
. . . zu
word das Wort, -e *or* ⹀er
work die Arbeit; das Werk, -e
work arbeiten; (*mechanically*) funktionieren
world die Welt
write schreiben, schrieb, geschrieben
writer der Schriftsteller, -
wrong falsch

year das Jahr, -e
yesterday gestern
yet doch; not yet noch nicht
young jung

Index

Accusative: The case of a noun, adjective, or pronoun which indicates the direct object.

Adjective: A word that describes or modifies a noun or pronoun.

Adverb: A word that modifies a verb, an adjective, or another adverb.

Antecedent: The word to which a later word refers.

Auxiliary Verb: A verb which helps in the conjugation of another verb (he *has* left, you *must* leave).

Cardinal Number: A numeral which answers the question "How many?"

Case: The form of a noun, pronoun, or adjective which indicates its relationship to other words (nominative, genitive, dative, accusative).

Clause: A group of words containing a subject and predicate. A main (independent) clause can form a sentence in itself; a subordinate (dependent) clause can function only with an independent clause.

Comparison: The change in the form of an adjective or adverb showing degrees of quality: positive (*old*), comparative (*older*), superlative (*oldest*).

Conjugation: The inflections or changes of form in verbs showing tense, mood, voice, person, and number.

Conjunction: A word used to connect words, phrases, or clauses. Coordinating conjunctions connect expressions of equal value. Subordinating conjunctions connect a dependent clause with a main clause.

Dative: The case of a noun, adjective, or pronoun which makes it an indirect object.

Declension: The inflections or changes in a noun, pronoun, or adjective showing case, gender, and number.

Definite Article: der, die, das.

Der-Words: Words declined like the definite article.

Ein-Words: Words declined like the indefinite article.

Finite Verb: The conjugated (or inflected) verb form showing person, number, tense.

Gender: The grammatical distinction of nouns and pronouns (masculine, feminine, neuter).

Genitive: The case denoting a possessive relationship.

Imperative: The mood of a verb expressing a command.

Indefinite Article: ein, eine, ein.

Indicative: The mood of a verb expressing a fact.

Indirect Discourse: A statement that is merely reported, rather than quoted directly.

Indirect Question: A question in indirect discourse.

Infinitive: The form of the verb which expresses its general meaning without distinction as to grammatical person or number.

Inflect: To change the form of a word to indicate gender, number, case, person, tense, etc.

Interrogative: An adjective or a pronoun used to ask a direct or indirect question.

Intransitive Verb: A verb expressing an action or state that does not require a direct object.

Inversion: A reversal of the normal sequence: subject-verb.